Jordan L. Harding

COLLECTION

Class of
1950

Doctor of Laws (Honorary)
2002

SHENANDOAH
UNIVERSITY

The Revenger's Tragedy

Also by MacD. P. Jackson:

Shakespeare's "A Lover's Complaint": Its Date and Authenticity
Studies in Attribution: Middleton and Shakespeare

The Revenger's Tragedy

Attributed to Thomas Middleton

A Facsimile of the 1607/8 Quarto

Introduced by MacD. P. Jackson

Rutherford • Madison • Teaneck
Fairleigh Dickinson University Press
London and Toronto: Associated University Presses

© 1983 by Associated University Presses, Inc.

Associated University Presses, Inc.
4 Cornwall Drive
East Brunswick, NJ 08816

Associated University Presses Ltd
27 Chancery Lane
London WC2A 1NF, England

Associated University Presses
2133 Royal Windsor Drive
Unit 1
Mississauga, Ontario,
Canada L5J 1K5

ISBN 0-8386-3131-2

Library of Congress Catalog Card Number: 81-72052

Printed in the United States of America

CONTENTS

PREFACE

This facsimile of *The Revenger's Tragedy* has been printed, with permission, from the 1608 quarto (69682, STC 24150) in The Huntington Library, San Marino, California. I am grateful to the Librarian, the Curator of Rare Books, and the Huntington's photographic department.

The introduction, with its copious notes, will serve as a guide to scholarship on the play. A careful evaluation of evidence for the play's authorship has resulted in Middleton's name appearing on the title page—the first time it has done so in any published edition. The facsimile, besides making *The Revenger's Tragedy* generally available in the form in which it appeared before its Jacobean readers, will afford a means of checking those bibliographical, linguistic, and orthographical details which support the attribution to Middleton.

Sincere thanks are due to Dr. O. B. Hardison, Director of the Folger Shakespeare Library, who kindly arranged that photographs of the Folger copies of the quarto be provided (though, as it turned out, these were not used as the basis for this facsimile); to Professor George R. Price for sending me his list of quarto press variants and allowing me to reproduce it here; to Dr. Roger V. Holdsworth for giving me the details of his unpublished findings summarized on pages 29–30 below and for correcting and supplementing my introduction at two other points; to the editors of the *Papers of the Bibliographical Society of America* for permitting me to repeat some sentences from my article on the quarto of *The Revenger's Tragedy* in *PBSA* 75; to Mr. Thomas Yoseloff and the editorial staff of Associated University Presses, and the committee of Fairleigh Dickinson University Press; and to my wife, Nicole, who has helped with typing and proofreading.

INTRODUCTION

The Revenger's Tragedy brilliantly combines two of the most vital dramatic forms of its time, revenge tragedy and that strain of Jacobean satirical comedy in which knavish wits intrigue against no less knavish gulls in a world where orthodox values are subverted and moral lunacy presides. The play draws too on the Morality drama and on a vigorous medieval homiletic tradition, with its offshoots in literature and art. Yet its ironic treatment of a melodramatic plot gives it a tone akin to the "savage farce" that T. S. Eliot found in Marlowe's *The Jew of Malta.*[1] The play is a curious mixture of the passionate and the dispassionate; it is both hot and cold, but never warm, and by no means tepid.

It broods over death and corruption in poetry that entangles us in the rich complexity of its imagery. It titillates with its show of sexual depravity and involves us in its sadistic violence. We are made the willing accomplices of a self-appointed instrument of justice whose purity of motive is soon tainted by excessive delight in his task. Our warmer human sympathies are seldom aroused. But our frequent laugher at the ironic twists of the plot, the macabre jesting or complacent hypocrisy of the characters, the sardonic or self-congratulatory asides, the sheer bravura inventiveness of Vindice and his brother—and, beyond them, the author—is complicated by the reverberations of the oft-repeated words *sin, damnation, heaven, doom, devil, hell. The Revenger's Tragedy* has aptly been praised for "the consistency with which it achieves, not a moral superiority over lust and corruption, but an ability to realise and place its own attraction to them."[2] No Jacobean play outside the Shakespeare canon

9

has proved so fascinating to modern critics. Naturally, they would like to know who wrote it.

The play was first published anonymously in 1607/8. The traditional ascription to Cyril Tourneur derives from a play list appended to an edition of *The Old Law* published by Edward Archer in 1656. This is a thoroughly unreliable source of new attributions, and because *The Atheist's Tragedy,* the only extant play undoubtedly by Tourneur, is unlike *The Revenger's Tragedy* in many important respects, E. H. C. Oliphant challenged Archer's authority and in 1926 argued for Thomas Middleton's authorship.[3] He thus initiated a lively controversy that still persists.

It would be disingenuous of me to pretend to be an impartial commentator on this debate; indeed, the present facsimile has been prepared with a view to familiarizing scholars with the nature of the evidence that has been accumulated in support of Oliphant's claim. Most recent editors of *The Revenger's Tragedy* have been agnostic on the question of authorship; their agnosticism has had the practical result of allowing tradition, or perhaps we should call it habit, to prevail, so that Tourneur's name appears on cover and title page. Here it is contended that the balance of probabilities so strongly favors Middleton's authorship of the play that it is more reasonable to attribute it to him than either to return it to its initial anonymity or to adopt Archer's conjecture. But this introduction will deal first with matters of text and date.

Text

The sole seventeenth-century text of *The Revenger's Tragedy* is a quarto printed and published by George Eld and dated 1607 in some copies, 1608 in others; title pages of this edition vary only in the single digit.[4] Eld had entered the play in the Stationers' Register on 7 October 1607, along with Middleton's *A Trick to Catch the Old One,* which he printed on the same stock of paper and in the same font of type.[5] *A Trick,* of which all copies are dated 1608, also exhibits variant title pages, the first anonymous, but the second including an ascription to "T.M."

Twenty-four copies of the quarto of *The Revenger's Tragedy*

10

are known to me, only twelve of which were listed in Greg's *Bibliography*. They are as follows: British Library (three copies); Victoria and Albert Museum (two copies); Bodleian (two copies, one lacking sheet B); Worcester College, Oxford; King's College, Cambridge; Dulwich College, London; National Library of Scotland; Sir Israel Gollancz; Boston Public Library; Folger (two copies); Chapin; Huntington (two copies); Yale (two copies); Harvard; Princeton; Texas Christian University; William Andrews Clark Library. George R. Price collated seven American copies *literatim* and undertook or obtained partial collations of two others. R. A. Foakes checked four British copies,[6] and in preparing the present facsimile I have consulted in addition the two Bodleian Library copies and the two copies in the Victoria and Albert Museum. Allardyce Nicoll had earlier examined the Gollancz copy, not collated by Price, Foakes, or myself.[7]

Price found twenty-nine stop-press corrections, eighteen of them in sheet H, of which inner and outer formes are both variant, others in A(o), D(i), E(i), F(o), and G(o). H(o) exists in three states. Most variants involve trivial corrections of literals, faulty spacing, or mispunctuation, but some of those in H are more substantial and appear to have been made with reference to the manuscript. A complete list of variants so far detected is given at the end of this volume. Most editors have regarded the change on H4v of "beast" to "brest" as a miscorrection, but J. C. Maxwell plausibly defended "mad brest" as a possible compound on the analogy of "mad-brain."[8]

The quarto has the following skeleton pattern:

	A	B	C	D	E	F	G	H	I
Outer formes:	I	II	III	II	III	II	III	II	II
Inner formes:	II	I	IV	I	IV	I	IV	I	I

This implies a two-skeleton method of printing, adapted to the use of two presses for the central section of the quarto. The stints of two compositors can be distinguished by their contrasting habits in the spacing of punctuation and in the spelling of certain words.[9]

Compositor X preferred not to space colons, semicolons, question marks, and exclamation marks. He abbreviated speech prefixes for the Duke and Duchess to *Duk* and *Duc(h)*, and omitted the "t" from *Duches(se)* in stage directions and dialogue. He did not capitalize *diuill* or its variants. He often used "y" spellings in *ynough* and *yfaith*, and tolerated *e'm*. He avoided the use of the apostrophe in *tis*, *twas*, and *twere*. He usually set long "s" before "k", and he was responsible for all the many colons and semicolons that end speeches.

Compositor Y preferred to space colons, semicolons, question marks, and exclamation marks, though he was inconsistent in his treatment of punctuation within the line (rather than at line endings). He used the full *Duke* for speech prefixes, and the abbreviation *Dut(ch)* for the Duchess, also including the "t" in *Dutches(se)* in stage directions and dialogue. He alone employed the full form *Mother* in speech prefixes. He capitalized *Diuill* and its variants, and avoided "y" spellings in *inough* (or *enough*) and *ifaith*. He frequently set the apostrophe in *'tis, 'twas,* and *'twere;* and he was far more tolerant than Compositor X of "-ie" endings. He set only short "s" before "k".

Compositor Y appears to have set A2, B1–B2v, D1–D2v, E1–E2, E4v, F3–G2v, H3–H3v, H4v, I1v, I2v; and Compositor X the rest of the text. Such a compositorial division of labor can be related to the skeleton pattern: over the middle section of the quarto, when two presses were in operation, the compositors shared the typesetting equally; at the beginning and end of the quarto Compositor X did the bulk of the typesetting for a single press.

The workmanship of the same two men can be traced in many play quartos printed by Eld around 1607/8. As they each set typically Middletonian contractions, colloquial forms, and spellings only in *The Revenger's Tragedy* and in plays of Middleton's undoubted or probable authorship, and adhered to the known orthographical preferences of other dramatists in setting their plays, we can be confident that the Middletonian linguistic pattern of *The Revenger's Tragedy* is not a product of the printing house.

There are many indications that the quarto, which presents few major textual cruxes, was printed from the author's holograph.[10] Many exits and entrances are not marked, and the stage directions generally seem too erratic to derive from a promptbook, while the descriptive nature of several points to the playwright. There is no sign of theatrical annotation anticipating the need for properties or sound effects. The frequent use of mere numerals as speech prefixes for certain minor characters might confuse a prompter or a scribe preparing actors' parts, especially in Act V, scene i, where "1" and "2" are made to stand for two different pairs of persons. A problem over speech prefixes in the final scene has excited a good deal of comment.[11]

The lineation of the verse is inconsistent. It appears that in the manuscript from which the quarto was printed prose and verse were not always clearly distinguished. Both compositors were especially perplexed by the frequent abrupt transitions from one medium to another, even within a single speech. The incorporation of ordinary speech rhythms into the verse and the natural tendency of the prose to fall into irregular iambics were further sources of confusion. Moreover, the author was apt to "precede or interrupt blank verse patterns with short hypermetrical lines."[12] The outcome is that editorial arrangements of the dialogue may differ over points of detail, though there has been no appreciable divergence in the treatment of the longer verse speeches. The matter is fully discussed by R. A. Foakes in his introduction to the Revels edition.

It would seem likely, then, that the quarto was set from authorial "foul papers" in Greg's broad sense of the term—holograph clean enough to serve as basis for a transcript to be used in the theater, but not carefully prepared by the playwright with publication in mind.[13] The evidence that this manuscript was in Middleton's hand will be considered in the section on authorship.

Sources and Date

Given the ingenious intricacies of its plot, which would furnish material for half a dozen more conventional tragedies, it is not surprising that no single narrative source for the action of *The Revenger's Tragedy* has been discovered. But analogues to certain of its situations and incidents have been found in tales of Italian villainy: in the story of Alessandro de' Medici, whose assassination in 1537 was narrated as the twelfth novel of the second day in the *Heptameron* of Margueritte of Navarre, of which an English version was included in William Painter's *The Palace of Pleasure* (1567); in Giraldi Cinthio's *Hecatommithi* (1567), the most pertinent story having been freely translated by Barnaby Rich in his *Farewell to Military Profession* (1581); and, more doubtfully, in accounts of the Este family in Matteo Bandello's *Novelle* (1554) and elsewhere. The episode in *The Revenger's Tragedy*, II.iii, in which the enraged Lussurioso, sword drawn, is disconcerted to find the Duchess in bed with the Duke rather than with his bastard, Spurio, has been traced to Book I of Heliodorus's *Aethiopia*, rendered in English as *An Aethiopian History* (1587) by Thomas Underdowne, and as Ross has pointed out, the rape of Antonio's lady and the subsequent revenge by the company of lords have an obvious antecedent in the widely known story of the rape of Lucrece. John Florio's *A World of Words* (1598) provides a gloss on the play's descriptive Italian names.[14]

The play's indebtedness to the various dramatic conventions of its time has already been mentioned. Its author's fascination with *Hamlet*, among revenge tragedies, seems certain, and the influence of *Volpone*, among satiric comedies, is probable. The parallels with Middleton's city comedies of 1602–1606 might, of course, be explained in more than one way. Commentators have also noted possible connections with Shakespeare's *King Lear*, Marston's *The Malcontent*, *The Fawn*, and *Antonio's Revenge*, and Chettle's *Hoffman*, among plays written within the first few years of the seventeenth century. The incident in *The Revenger's Tragedy*, III.iv, in which Junior Brother defies his gaolers in the vain expectation that his execution will be stayed and his release contrived by his brothers and the Duke, may have been inspired by *The Spanish Tragedy*, III.vi, in which Pedringano entertains similarly baseless hopes. There were reprints of *The Spanish Tragedy* in 1599 and, with problematical additions, in 1602, when the title page claimed that the enlarged play had "of late been divers times acted."

These debts and relationships have suggested that *The Reven-*

ger's Tragedy was written about 1605/6, though early 1607 is possible.

Authorship: External Evidence for Tourneur

External evidence of the authorship of *The Revenger's Tragedy* is meager and inconclusive. Edward Archer attributed the play to "Tournour" in his *Old Law* catalogue of 1656. Greg, in the course of a thorough and scrupulous evaluation of the seventeenth-century play lists, calculated that at least two out of every three of Archer's new attributions that can be checked were "careless blunders or irresponsible guesses."[15] Of six further attributions that rest primarily on Archer's authority, none except that of *The Revenger's Tragedy* to Tourneur has won significant acceptance.

The attribution to Tourneur thus originated in the kind of external testimony which, as Oliphant noted, "is treated with contempt in some other cases."[16] Bentley goes as far as to assert in connection with Archer's attribution of *The Country Girl* to Thomas Brewer that "the attributions of this list have no authority."[17] Francis Kirkman's repetition of Archer's ascription (which he expanded to "Cyrill Tourneur") is without independent value, since his catalogues of 1661 and 1671 were based on those of his predecessors and repeat obvious blunders, as Greg noted.[18] Although Tourneur's relative obscurity means that he is not a dramatist whose name would normally have attracted erroneous seventeenth-century ascriptions, Archer's crediting of *The Revenger's Tragedy* to the author of *The Atheist's Tragedy* "may rest on no more than similarity of title," the obvious cause of his misattribution of *Every Woman in her Humour* to Jonson.[19] Archer seems to have had no special prejudice in favor of the famous; his mistakes included the assignment of *Love's Labour's Lost* to the obscure William Sampson, and he made new and incorrect ascriptions to such little-known writers as Lewis Machin, Thomas Goffe, and Ludovic Lloyd.

Bentley's comment on *The Country Girl* is perhaps too dismissive of Archer, who shows occasional signs of "unexpected knowledge,"[20] but the external evidence that Tourneur wrote *The Revenger's Tragedy* is worth very little indeed.

15

We have seen that *The Revenger's Tragedy* was registered in conjunction with Middleton's *A Trick to Catch the Old One.* David J. Lake asserts that on the Stationers' Register "there is no instance of the coupling of plays known to be by different authors through the entire Elizabethan and Jacobean periods," although there are several couplings of plays by the same author, including *Sejanus* and *Volpone* (without mention of Jonson's name).[21]

Lake adds that in his commendatory verses to *Women Beware Women,* Nathaniel Richards, a "Familiar Acquaintance" of Middleton, uses a phrase from *The Revenger's Tragedy;* the echo must have been conscious, because into his own tragedy *Messalina* he inserts the whole line of which the phrase is a part. It would be a reasonable inference that while praising *Women Beware Women* Richards intended a glancing allusion to another play that he knew to be Middleton's.

Again, these are far from compelling considerations, but they cannot be dismissed as worthless. On the external evidence the claims of Tourneur and Middleton seem roughly equivalent.

Against Middleton's candidacy it has been urged that around 1604 to 1607 he was writing city comedies for the boy actors to perform at private theaters, whereas the anonymous play is a revenge tragedy said on the title page to have been performed by the King's Men, presumably at the Globe. However, the belief that stage effects called for in the text prove that *The Revenger's Tragedy* was written specially for the Globe has been shown to rest on a misunderstanding, and there are even reasons for mistrusting George Eld's claim that it was acted by the King's Men.[22] But acceptance of Eld's title page at face value would not prejudice the case for Middleton; he had certainly worked on tragedies in the early years of the seventeenth century, he was throughout his career an "unattached" playwright, one of "the rather prolific professionals who [appear] never to have had any long sustained company attachment, but to have sold [their] plays here and there," and an early association between Middleton and the King's Men, however noncommittal on both sides, may be deduced on quite independent grounds.[23] And if it makes critical sense to view *The Revenger's Tragedy* as merging the genres of Jacobean city comedy and revenge tragedy, Middleton's success as a comic satirist during the years immediately preceding the publication of *The Revenger's Tragedy* can scarcely militate against his claim to the play.

There is no evidence to connect Tourneur with the King's Men before (or after) 23 February 1612, when his lost play, *The Nobleman,* was performed by them. In fact, there is nothing to suggest that he wrote for the stage at all before composing *The Atheist's Tragedy,* now usually dated about 1610.[24]

Internal Evidence

Internal evidence cited in the controversy over authorship falls into two main categories. Every quantifiable and objective test involving details of language, syntax, meter, or orthography has pointed to Middleton's authorship.[25] The case for Tourneur has rested on literary arguments: it has been contended that *The Revenger's Tragedy* and *The Atheist's Tragedy* are similar and un-Middletonian in their concern with revenge, in their moral atmosphere, in their use of poetic imagery, and in their conception and construction "as entities."

The Case for Tourneur

The best attempt to associate *The Revenger's Tragedy* with *The Atheist's Tragedy* and dissociate it from Middleton's dramatic and poetic practices is by Inga-Stina Ekeblad (now Ewbank).[26] She offers a good critical account of *The Revenger's Tragedy,* showing how the author has assimilated into a perfect unity elements previously separate in the dramatic tradition. But in explaining why *The Atheist's Tragedy* lacks the intensity and coherence of the earlier play, in denying any informing moral purpose to Middleton's comedies, and in viewing the dramatic concerns and methods of *The Changeling* and *Women Beware Women* as too different in kind from those of *The Revenger's Tragedy* for Mid-

17

dleton's authorship of the anonymous play to be possible, she is hardly convincing.

In my opinion, the "uncompromising moral sense" that Oliphant found in the author of *The Revenger's Tragedy* is, as he went on to remark, complicated by "that love of the disgusting that is the hallmark of your true missionary moralist";[27] the same ambivalence characterizes Middleton's work; the quality of mind displayed by Tourneur in *The Atheist's Tragedy* is incompatible with his having written *The Revenger's Tragedy* such a short time before; and, given Middleton's extraordinary versatility and the potent influence of *Hamlet* on *The Revenger's Tragedy* and of *Macbeth* on *The Changeling*,[28] Middleton's later tragedies are a natural enough development from the preoccupations and the dramatic language of *The Revenger's Tragedy*, written, it should be noted, over fifteen years earlier. Quoting from the speeches in which De Flores forces Beatrice-Joanna to recognize the inescapable consequences of her unthinking employment of his services, Ekeblad says: "It is language aiming at psychological re-creation of characters' minds, not at emphatic communication of moral truth."[29] Surely it is Middleton's achievement to have evolved a language that succeeds triumphantly in performing both functions at once.

The issues raised here are of obvious interest and importance, and Ekeblad's article is a useful contribution to critical dialogue, but as a case for authorship it is vitiated by its subjectivity. Whether the dramatic and intellectual qualities of *The Revenger's Tragedy* are more or less Tourneuresque than Middletonian is a question well worth debating, but competent critics have given it opposing answers. Students of Middleton who know his work well have felt quite able to accommodate *The Revenger's Tragedy* within their conception of his development.[30] Even the common notion that *The Revenger's Tragedy* displays a Tourneuresque "moral passion" of which Middleton is free has been repudiated by some critics. Felix E. Schelling found *The Revenger's Tragedy* lacking "the well-defined moral intent" of *The Atheist's Tragedy*, while David M. Holmes has devoted a whole book to the proposition that, despite the bland surface of his comedies, Middleton is a thor-

18

oughgoing moralist at heart.[31] If Holmes may be accused of misrepresenting the nature of Middleton's art, the account of *The Revenger's Tragedy* in which Irving Ribner assimilates it to the orthodox piety of *The Atheist's Tragedy* seems no less a distortion of the complexities of our response. The seventeenth-century audience of *The Revenger's Tragedy* would leave the theater, he concludes, "with that particular sense of the imperfection and impermanence of worldly things which leads naturally to contemplation of the perfect life to come."[32] Might not their pious musings have been tainted by an element of vicarious pleasure in the ingenious savagery with which Vindice and Hippolito torture the vicious duke, or by laughter at the shrugging good humor with which the brothers accept their final *peripeteia?* My own response to the play more nearly resembles that of a child at a Punch and Judy show than that of a religious zealot at a sermon.

A most impressive list of structural and thematic parallels between *The Revenger's Tragedy* and *The Atheist's Tragedy* was compiled by W. T. Jewkes, who commented: "Almost any single one of the above parallel incidents, scenes, characters, motifs, even themes in these two plays can be further paralleled in other plays of the period. But the sum total of similarities is a matter of some weight, and, even more so, the especial complementariness with which they are treated in these two plays."[33] These parallels, insofar as they require explanation, may be seen as pointing not to common authorship—any more than do those between *The Revenger's Tragedy* and *Hamlet*—but to Tourneur's familiarity with the earlier play. I imagine that he wrote *The Atheist's Tragedy* partly in reaction to *The Revenger's Tragedy,* and deliberately echoed its title. In fact, Jewkes's point is that critics can usually find means of rationalizing whatever initial decision they make about the play's authorship. The list of parallels, he says, "really proves nothing . . . except that starting from a basic assumption of common or of different authorship will in most cases produce the evidence necessary to support whichever of the two assumptions the student of the play began with." He concludes that "arguments for the authorship of Elizabethan plays based on any kind of internal

19

evidence alone are necessarily suspect, and probably a waste of time." But such total skepticism is unwarranted. Arguments based on literary-critical and interpretative considerations have led to opposite conclusions and must hence be admitted to have too large a subjective component to serve the purposes of demonstration,[34] but other forms of internal evidence are not vulnerable to this stricture. Tests based on quantifiable features of style and orthography have all given the same unequivocal answer.

The Case for Middleton

Oliphant's case for Middleton's authorship of *The Revenger's Tragedy* was supported by his usual haphazard collection of internal "clues"—verbal parallels with the undoubted plays of Middleton, locutions that he especially favored, and tricks of style said to be typical of him. Over the next few decades similar items of internal evidence were cited by several scholars, whose work was summarized by Samuel Schoenbaum.[35] The chief defect in most of these studies lay in their failure to make the negative check necessary to demonstrate that Middleton "peculiarities" were genuinely peculiar.

Middleton: Linguistic Evidence

The first systematically to apply modern techniques to the problem of the play's authorship was Peter B. Murray, who undertook, in modified form, the kind of investigation that Cyrus Hoy had so impressively conducted on the "Beaumont and Fletcher" plays.[36] Hoy showed that Jacobean dramatists differed in their characteristic "linguistic patterns"—in their habits with respect to certain word forms and colloquial contractions, such as *doth, 'em, ye, i'th, h'as, a* (for *he*), *ha', 'tas, d'ee*—and that their preferences sufficiently survived the whims of scribes and compositors for all Massinger's unaided plays, for example, to be easily distinguished, on this basis, from all Fletcher's, and the shares of the two dramatists in their collaborative works to be clearly defined.

20

Murray examined the linguistic forms in *The Revenger's Tragedy,* in *The Atheist's Tragedy,* in five plays by Middleton (*Your Five Gallants, A Trick to Catch the Old One, A Mad World My Masters, The Phoenix,* and *A Game at Chess*—the first four roughly contemporary with *The Revenger's Tragedy* and representing the work of four printers altogether, the last chosen because it is preserved in a manuscript in Middleton's own hand), in five control plays written by other authors but printed, like *The Revenger's Tragedy,* by George Eld in 1607/8, and in Jonson's *The Alchemist* (1612), a product of Thomas Snodham's printing house, from which *The Atheist's Tragedy* had emerged at the end of 1611. He performed separate analyses for preferred linguistic forms and preferred spellings of them, presenting his data in five tables. Table 1 records the spelling of the forms studied, *w'are* and *we're,* for example, being counted as different spellings of the contraction for *we are;* in Table 2 variant spellings such as *w'are* and *we're* are combined indiscriminately, and the relevant distinction is between use and nonuse of a contracted form.

Analysis of Table 1 revealed that "in every one of the eighteen spelling conflicts between Tourneur and Middleton the pattern of spellings occurring in *RT* is closer to Middleton's than to Tourneur's." The possibility that this result is a matter of chance is, statistically speaking, so remote that it can confidently be dismissed. Murray examined all forms of a preselected type, so that bias in the handling of the data seems to have been avoided; and, as he insisted, "There can be no doubt that spelling is sub-stylistic and therefore not subject to change as a writer moves from poetry to prose or from tragedy to comedy,"[37] so that the disparity between *The Revenger's Tragedy* and *The Atheist's Tragedy* and the similarity between *The Revenger's Tragedy* and Middleton's plays cannot be explained away on literary grounds.

Richard Proudfoot's detailed strictures upon Murray's case largely ignored spelling evidence and concentrated on the data concerning use or avoidance of the contractions themselves.[38] He argued that the range of figures covering the five representative Middleton plays was for most contractions so wide that no

21

sure conclusions could be drawn. But when correct methods of comparison are adopted the variation among Middleton plays proves to be unimportant. Each of the five more closely matches *The Revenger's Tragedy* than does *The Atheist's Tragedy* in the use of contractions, and for four of the plays this greater congruity reaches statistical significance.[39]

Defenders of Archer's ascription have drawn attention to the disclaimer whereby Murray justified his inclusion of a chapter on *The Revenger's Tragedy* in his book on Tourneur: "So long as we study this problem from a text at least one remove from the author's papers, we can never do more than establish the *probability* of authorship by means of linguistic and spelling tests, and that probability is only as good as the inferences about scribes and compositors upon which it is based."[40] But Murray was simply straining to extricate himself from a dilemma. He had shown that *The Revenger's Tragedy* was probably written by Middleton; yet a book on Tourneur would hardly be worth publishing if he could not include a chapter on *The Revenger's Tragedy*, upon which, moreover, he had good critical remarks to make. As a reason for distrusting his own case, the quoted sentence is quite inadequate. Whatever texts we were studying and whatever the forms of evidence they were to yield, we would still be dealing only in "probabilities" in assigning authors, as in all human matters. Even a holograph manuscript with the playwright's signature at the end could not provide *absolute* certainty, for the playwright might have been a mere copyist and the signature might be a forgery. And although there are firm grounds for believing that the compositors who set *The Revenger's Tragedy* in George Eld's printing house and those who set *The Atheist's Tragedy* in Thomas Snodham's all reproduced fairly faithfully the linguistic character of their copy,[41] Murray's tests do not really require any initial assumptions about scribal or compositorial practices. Rather, Murray's data themselves, as supplemented by the studies of Price, Lake, and myself, shortly to be described, virtually compel us to conclude that those who transmitted the text of *The Revenger's Tragedy* preserved the linguistic character of the author's original manuscript and that this manuscript was Middleton's, for any compositorial or scribal corruption ought to have been random in its effect. It is

22

incredible that agents in the transmission of the text would have altered forms exclusively in the direction of agreement between *The Revenger's Tragedy* and Middleton's plays and of disagreement between these plays and everybody else's, including Tourneur's *The Atheist's Tragedy*.

Further linguistic data have been added to Murray's. Two independent studies have each exhaustively compared Middleton's thirteen unaided plays with a control corpus of well over one hundred plays by other early seventeenth-century dramatists, and shown that *The Revenger's Tragedy* exhibits a distinctively Middletonian linguistic pattern found in no other dramatist of the period. In its use of contractions and other such forms *The Revenger's Tragedy* is Middletonian to a degree equaled by no extant non-Middleton play of the period 1600–1625.[42]

I have elsewhere recorded the rates at which six contractions to which Middleton was especially partial occur in Middleton's plays, in one hundred early seventeenth-century plays by all the other main dramatists of the period, and in disputed plays, including *The Revenger's Tragedy*.[43] For each of these six contractions (*I'm, I'd, I've, on't, ne'er, e'en*) the figure for *The Revenger's Tragedy* is much closer to the Middleton than to the non-Middleton average, and the combined total of one hundred and four in *The Revenger's Tragedy* is close to the Middleton average total of ninety and far beyond the average non-Middleton total of sixteen. The highest non-Middleton total for the six contractions is fifty-five in Ben Jonson's *Bartholomew Fair*, apart from which only William Rowley's *A Woman Never Vexed* has a total (fifty-three) that exceeds the lowest Middleton total of forty-three. Most of Middleton's thirteen plays are close to his average. *The Revenger's Tragedy* further resembles the typical Middleton play in using the contractions *y', 'em, sh'as, 'tas, thou'rt, they're,* and enclitic *'t* at an above-average rate, and in its tendency to avoid such favorites of other dramatists as the formal *hath* and *doth, ye, a* (meaning *he*), *d'ee, t'ee, t'* before a vowel, *i'* for *in* (except in *i'th'*), *of't,* and the variants *o'the, 'hem,* and *'um*. There has not yet been discovered a non-Middleton play that shares these features.

George R. Price, who has been studying Middleton play

quartos for many years, showed that the quarto of *The Revenger's Tragedy* was in other respects consistent with its having been set from a manuscript in Middleton's own hand, and a long list has since been compiled of spelling links between the quarto and Middleton's holograph of *A Game at Chess*, written more than fifteen years later.[44] One highly significant link between the *Revenger's Tragedy* quarto and the Trinity MS of *A Game at Chess* has only recently been noted. In *The Revenger's Tragedy* four stage directions are punctuated with quite meaningless question marks: "*Enter* Ambitioso, *and* Superuacuo?" (E2v), "*Enter* Ambitioso, *and* Superuacuo? *with officers.*" (E3), "*The Reuengers daunce?*" (I3v), and "*Enter the other Maske of entended murderers?*" (I3v). These anomalies in punctuation can neatly be explained as originating in Middleton's peculiar addiction to a mark resembling the medieval *punctus elevatus,* which Bald transcribed three times as an exclamation mark when it occurred in stage directions of the *Game at Chess* holograph, and which was printed four times as an exclamation mark and three times as a question mark in stage directions of Middleton quartos—*Your Five Gallants* (A3v), *Michaelmas Term* (A2), *A Trick to Catch the Old One* (E1v), and *Honourable Entertainments* (C8v, D1v, D2v, and D5)—and once as a question mark in a stage direction of *The Puritan* (G2v), a play almost certainly by Middleton.[45]

In a review of one of the studies of the Middleton canon mentioned above, R. A. Foakes concedes that the evidence adduced by Price, Murray, and Lake appears to show that the copy for the original quarto of *The Revenger's Tragedy* was a Middleton holograph, but points out that "to establish Middleton as the writer of the manuscript behind the printed text is not the same thing as to establish that he wrote the play." Middleton may have been "the transcriber of another man's work."[46]

There are compelling reasons for rejecting this as a serious possibility, quite apart from the unlikely coincidence that would be involved in Middleton's having copied out a Tourneur play first suspected to be Middleton's on purely literary grounds by critics who could not have foreseen recent bibliographical findings, and the bizarre logic that would plead the lack of a

24

documented connection between Middleton and the King's Men during the period when *The Revenger's Tragedy* was written, and then posit the company's employment of him as theatrical scribe.

Irregularities and ambiguities of presentation in the quarto suggest that it was set from "foul papers"; had Middleton been transcribing a Tourneur holograph we would expect him to have produced a manuscript at least as orderly as the much more consistent and careful holograph that seems to have served as copy for the quarto of *The Atheist's Tragedy*. Moreover, although Middleton as transcriber might have imposed his own *spelling* preferences upon another man's play, he could hardly have altered its whole linguistic character without thoroughly revising its dialogue. The monosyllabic contractions in *The Revenger's Tragedy* fit the meter, as the uncontracted forms would not, and Middleton's liking for *on't*, for example (which appears eighteen times in *The Revenger's Tragedy*, twenty-two times in the average Middleton play, four times in the average non-Middleton play, and only once in *The Atheist's Tragedy*), is a liking not merely for a certain spelling but for a turn of phrase that can incorporate this contraction; the collocation *on it* does not appear in *The Atheist's Tragedy* at all, and *of it* (which *on't* more often stands for) appears only three times, so a copyist could not possibly introduce *on't* into *The Atheist's Tragedy* with a Middletonian frequency by mere adjustment to the orthography.[47]

Middleton: Oaths and Exclamations

An even more important point is that the Middletonian pattern of contractions and so on in *The Revenger's Tragedy* is only one of several types of objective evidence pointing to Middleton's authorship of the play. For example, a comprehensive survey of all oaths, exclamations, and other expletives used in each of Middleton's undoubted plays, in a control corpus of one hundred plays by his contemporaries and in disputed and collaborative plays linked with Middleton, reveals that Middleton's partiality for some and avoidance of others are so individual that eight of his plays (including the first seven) can confidently be separated from all the non-Middleton plays on this basis alone; *The Revenger's Tragedy* unequivocally belongs with the eight most distinctive Middleton plays.[48]

Eleven rare expletives are at least ten times more frequent in Middleton's than in the non-Middleton plays. Middleton's eight most distinctive plays use them thirteen to thirty times; sixty-seven of the one hundred non-Middleton plays (including *The Atheist's Tragedy*) do not use them at all, and only one play affords as many as five instances. The total for *The Revenger's Tragedy* is fourteen. Middleton uses a further twenty-eight expletives significantly more often than his fellow dramatists. The eight especially distinctive Middleton plays use nineteen to twenty-four of these expletives at least once; no non-Middleton play uses more than eighteen, and the average is eight, but the total for *The Revenger's Tragedy* is twenty-one. Further, *The Revenger's Tragedy*, unlike *The Atheist's Tragedy*, is remarkably free from expletives avoided by Middleton but favored by other dramatists. No non-Middleton play of 1600–1625 is so Middletonian in its expletives as is *The Revenger's Tragedy*.

Middleton: Function Words

A statistical analysis of the rates at which thirteen high-frequency function words (such as *and, it, of, to, a*) occur in *The Revenger's Tragedy*, in Middleton's plays, and in sixty non-Middleton plays, yields similar, though less decisive results.[49] When rates for *The Revenger's Tragedy* are compared by a standard mathematical measure to rates for each of the other plays in turn, and plays are ranked in order of the closeness to which their rates match those of *The Revenger's Tragedy*, three Middleton plays head the list, and all the Middleton plays are more highly ranked than *The Atheist's Tragedy*. The high ranking of Middleton plays is statistically significant, the probability being considerably less than one in ten thousand that it is due to chance. Also statistically significant (with a chance probability of less than one in fifty) is the tendency, among Middleton's plays, for chronological proximity to *The Revenger's Tragedy* to correlate with closeness of fit in respect of function word rates—a tendency of which there is no trace whatsoever amongst the non-Middleton plays. This last finding makes perfectly good sense if Middleton wrote *The Revenger's Tragedy;* it seems inexplicable if Tourneur was the author.

The value of function-word frequencies as indicators of authorship has long been established; and for the investigation summarized here all contractions were expanded into their component parts (*to'th'* being counted as *to the,* for example), so that this evidence is entirely independent of the evidence of linguistic forms and strongly confirmatory of it.

Middleton: Meter

One further internal indicator of authorship deserves detailed consideration. Metrically the verse of *The Revenger's Tragedy* is completely unlike that of *The Atheist's Tragedy,* but very like that of Middleton's comedies of about 1602–1606. An essential and obvious difference between *The Atheist's Tragedy,* on the one hand, and *The Revenger's Tragedy* and the Middleton plays, on the other, lies in the treatment of line endings.[50] The verse of *The Revenger's Tragedy* is, like Middleton's, predominantly end-stopped, but has a high percentage of feminine endings; the verse of *The Atheist's Tragedy* has few feminine endings but many run-on lines, including a fair proportion of that extreme kind in which a phrasal unit occupies the end of one line and the beginning of the next. The difference is readily quantifiable, and Tourneur's poems, written both before and after *The Atheist's Tragedy,* exhibit the same idiosyncratic prosody as his play. As Lake insists, to accept Tourneur's authorship of *The Revenger's Tragedy* one would have to make the implausible assumption that "he totally abandoned his own verse style at some point between 1600 and 1606 in favour of a perfect imitation of Middleton's; and then re-accentuated his earlier tendencies in time for Vere's death in 1609," when he wrote a funeral poem with characteristically brutal enjambments.[51]

Minor variation among editorial arrangements of the verse of *The Revenger's Tragedy* cannot affect the conclusion that it is Middletonian rather than Tourneuresque.

27

Other metrical data, which most scholars have overlooked, reinforce this verdict. Ants Oras investigated pause patterns in the verse of English Renaissance drama, and subjected his findings to subtle and sensitive analysis.[52] His concern was with pauses in the blank verse line—their incidence in each of the nine possible positions in relation to the total number of pauses. As Oras, following a hint from Chambers, asserted: "Authors may deliberately choose to use little or much pausation in their verse, but they will generally be less aware of the positions in the line in which they pause. . . . the total patterns are likely to reveal much over which the person concerned has little or no control, almost as people are unable to control their cardiograms."[53] His numerous graphs support this suggestion: though general chronological trends in pause patterns mark a changing "rhythmic climate," playwrights can be seen to respond in their markedly individual ways. Oras counted (a) all pauses indicated by internal punctuation in the original editions, (b) all pauses other than commas so indicated, and (c) breaks caused by division of the iambic pentameter line between two characters. This third kind of "pause," rare before 1600, is of special significance because examples of its use are entirely authorial, unaffected by the habits of scribes or compositors.

Oras pointed out that the pause patterns of *The Revenger's Tragedy,* though compatible with those of Middleton's early comedies, were completely unlike those of *The Atheist's Tragedy.*[54] But his figures point even more clearly to Middleton's authorship of *The Revenger's Tragedy* than he realizes. His analysis of line split divisions (type c pauses) is based on figures and graphs for two hundred and sixteen plays. Authors include Shakespeare, Chapman, Marston, Jonson, Dekker, Heywood, Day, Fletcher, Massinger, Beaumont, Middleton, Rowley, Webster, Tourneur, Ford, Brome, Shirley, and Davenant. Graphs show the percentage of line-splits in each of the nine positions. An appropriate mathematical measure of the degree to which the other graphs match that for *The Revenger's Tragedy* is the Pearson product moment correlation, using the raw figures. Each of Middleton's thirteen unaided plays provides a closer fit to *The Revenger's Tragedy* than does *The Atheist's Tragedy.* Closest

28

of all is *A Trick to Catch the Old One*, the very play that was coupled with *The Revenger's Tragedy* in the Stationers' Register entry of 1607. When all two hundred and fifteen plays are matched against *The Revenger's Tragedy*, four of the best dozen matchings prove to be with Middleton plays.[55] If one were attempting to select a likely author for *The Revenger's Tragedy* solely on the evidence of its pause patterns, Middleton would be a natural choice of candidate.

Middleton: New Evidence

Middleton's authorship of *The Revenger's Tragedy* is the most probable explanation of some as yet unpublished findings made by R. V. Holdsworth of the University of Manchester in the course of an investigation into the problems of *Timon of Athens* and *Macbeth*. Holdsworth checked through the earliest available texts of all extant plays written in English between 1580 and 1642, a total of six hundred and forty-six plays surviving in six hundred and seventy-two texts, some of the plays having been preserved in more than one version. He discovered new indicators of Middleton's hand. The most notable are entrance directions in the exact form "Enter A (or A etc.) meeting B (or B etc.)." He found ten of these in Middleton's acknowledged plays and four in plays attributed to Middleton by Lake and Jackson, including an example in *The Revenger's Tragedy*, "*Enter the Bastard meeting the Dutchesse*" on F3v. Although a few such stage directions turn up in Caroline drama, the only other playwright to use several within the period 1602–1624 is Thomas Heywood. During those years, to which *The Revenger's Tragedy* and Middleton's plays belong, there are six examples in Heywood's undoubted plays, two in plays probably by him, and only two in the one hundred and ninety plays by other dramatists.

Holdsworth has also compiled figures for what he calls "interrogative repetition" in one hundred and ten plays, including all those by Middleton and most of those by dramatists writing during the first decade of the seventeenth century. He defines the stylistic device examined as "the exact repetition at the very beginning of a speech, or as the whole speech, of a word or phrase in the speech immediately preceding, so as to call attention to it in an interrogative or exclamatory way." He elaborates this basic definition so that it can be applied objectively and covers borderline cases. Middleton is especially given to the mannerism. When the one hundred and ten plays are ranked in terms of rate of use per thousand speeches, *The Puritan, The Revenger's Tragedy, A Chaste Maid in Cheapside, The Phoenix,* and *Women Beware Women* top the list, and five unquestioned Middleton plays are among the next ten.

Conclusion

Additional objective pointers to Middleton, miscellaneous in kind, are cited in a note.[56] They would in themselves suffice to raise a presumption of Middleton's authorship of *The Revenger's Tragedy*. By far the most impressive verbal parallel to any passage in *The Revenger's Tragedy* is afforded by a Middleton comedy of about the same period.

The investigator of problems of attribution must look for authorial "fingerprints"—features that, however inconsequential from a literary point of view, serve to identify an author by differentiating between his undoubted works and those of a wide range of writers contemporary with him and operating within the same genre. The "dark and ironical attitude towards life" which Allardyce Nicoll detected in both *The Revenger's Tragedy* and *The Atheist's Tragedy* is of little use as a means of identification;[57] nor can "mood, general temper and moral fervour" provide the requisite fingerprinting; though real enough, they "evade strict analysis," and are seen differently by critics with different temperaments and preoccupations.[58] Features that demonstrably do distinguish Middleton plays from all non-Middleton plays of 1600–1625 have, however, been discovered, and *The Revenger's Tragedy* bears these identifying marks.

Some scholars, regarding the evidence put forward on behalf of Tourneur and Middleton as hopelessly contradictory, have sought to return *The Revenger's Tragedy* to its original anonymity. But there is no conflict at all in the internal evidence that meets tolerable standards of objectivity. Disagreement arises only in those areas where, on any theory of authorship, we should expect it—areas encompassing the subjective responses of critics to the pertinent plays, and interpretation of the broad similarities and dissimilarities of outlook, method, and the like that have been discerned. And the external evidence, rightly assessed, is pretty evenly balanced, so that there is nothing to prevent us from provisionally accepting the overwhelming verdict of the properly conducted internal tests.

The editors of a recent anthology conclude their remarks on *The Revenger's Tragedy:* "But even the most persuasive modern proponent of Middleton acknowledges that *The Revenger's Tragedy* has 'not been proved beyond question' to be his work. As that is so, best to leave it to Cyril Tourneur."[59] On these terms no mistaken attribution could ever be corrected. In requiring that the case for Middleton be proved "beyond question" before they discard Archer's ascription, Fraser and Rabkin are rejecting a very strong probability in favor of what on the available evidence must be accounted no better than a remote possibility. As an eminent social scientist has written in a very different context: "Perfection is not to be found in human affairs, and every scientist is aware of the limitations of individual studies; he learns to base his conclusions on the agreed findings of many less-than-perfect studies, each having different limitations, and subject to different criticisms."[60] Scholars concerned with problems of disputed authorship should take the same common-sense attitude. Individually the objective tests described above may have their "vulnerabilities,"[61] though these have been grossly exaggerated, but they are so diverse that their convergence upon the same conclusion cannot plausibly be explained away. For this reason *The Revenger's Tragedy* is here "attributed to Thomas Middleton."

NOTES

1. *Elizabethan Dramatists* (London, 1968 ed.), pp. 63–64. The essay on Marlowe was first published in 1919.

2. T. B. Tomlinson, "The Morality of Revenge: Tourneur's Critics," *Essays in Criticism* 10 (1960): 143.

3. "The Authorship of *The Revenger's Tragedy*," *Studies in Philology* 23 (1926): 157–68. He had hesitantly made the Middleton connection in "Problems of Authorship in Elizabethan Dramatic Literature," *Modern Philology* 8 (1911): 411–59. F. G. Fleay, *A Biographical Chronicle of the English Drama, 1559–1642* (London, 1891), 2: 264, 272, had judged *The Revenger's Tragedy* far superior to Tourneur's undoubted work and pronounced its meter "purely Websterian." This was not unreasonable, because Middleton and Webster are metrically similar. For surveys of the authorship controversy see Charles Forker, "Cyril Tourneur," in *The New Intellectuals: A Survey and Bibliography of Recent Studies in English Renaissance Drama* (Lincoln, Neb., 1977), ed. Terence P. Logan and Denzell S. Smith, pp. 268–71; Kenneth Tucker, *A Bibliography of Writings by and about John Ford and Cyril Tourneur* (Boston, 1977), pp. x–xiii, 133–34; Samuel Schuman, *Cyril Tourneur* (Boston, 1977), pp. 57–78. These scholars failed, however, to assess correctly the studies surveyed and they were unable to take account of recent work, mentioned below, by Lake and Jackson. Philip J. Ayres provides a sensible brief summary of the case for Middleton in his booklet paradoxically entitled *Tourneur: The Revenger's Tragedy* (London, 1977), pp. 57–62.

4. W. W. Greg, *A Bibliography of the English Printed Drama to the Restoration* (London, 1939–59), 1: 253.

5. George R. Price, "The Authorship and the Bibliography of *The Revenger's Tragedy*," *The Library*, 5th ser., 15 (1960): 262–77 (271–72); "The Early Editions of *A trick to catch the old one*," *The Library*, 5th ser., 22 (1967): 205–27 (205–6).

6. R. A. Foakes, ed., *The Revenger's Tragedy* (London, 1966), Revels Plays, p. 1v.

7. Allardyce Nicoll, ed., *The Works of Cyril Tourneur* (London, 1929), pp. 305–6.

8. "Two Notes on *The Revenger's Tragedy*," *Modern Language Review* 44 (1949): 545.

9. MacD. P. Jackson, "Compositorial Practices in *The Revenger's Tragedy*, 1607–08," *PBSA: Papers of the Bibliographical Society of America* 75 (1981): 157–

70. The article substantiates in detail all bibliographical statements made in this section of the introduction.

10. The matter is discussed by Price, "Authorship and Bibliography," pp. 263–70.

11. C. S. Napier, "*The Revenger's Tragedy*," *Times Literary Supplement*, 13 March 1937, p. 188; Clifford Leech, "A Speech-Heading in *The Reuengers Tragedie*," *Review of English Studies* 18 (1941): 335–36; Eugene M. Waith, "The Ascription of Speeches in *The Revenger's Tragedy*," *Modern Language Notes* 57 (1942): 119–21; R. G. Howarth, "Who's Who in *The Revenger's Tragedy*," in *A Pot of Gillyflowers: Studies and Notes* (Cape Town, 1964), pp. 70–71.

12. Lawrence J. Ross, ed., *The Revenger's Tragedy* (Lincoln, Neb., 1966), Regents Renaissance Drama Series, p. xxxi.

13. W. W. Greg, *The Shakespeare First Folio* (Oxford, 1955), pp. 108–37.

14. Sources and the debts mentioned in the following paragraph are discussed by Foakes, *The Revenger's Tragedy* Revels ed., pp. lxiii–lxix, and Ross, Regents ed., pp. xix–xxiii. Relevant articles are: Samuel Schoenbaum, "*The Revenger's Tragedy*: A Neglected Source," *Notes and Queries* 195 (1950): 338; N. W. Bawcutt, "*The Revenger's Tragedy* and the Medici Family," *Notes and Queries* 202 (1957): 192–93; G. K. Hunter, "A Source for *The Revenger's Tragedy*," *Review of English Studies*, n.s. 10 (1959): 181–82; Pierre Legouis, "Réflexions sur la recherche des sources à propos de la *Tragédie du Vengeur*," *Études Anglaises* 12 (1959): 47–55; L. G. Salingar, "*The Revenger's Tragedy*: Some Possible Sources," *Modern Language Review* 60 (1965): 3–12; J. W. Lever, *The Tragedy of State* (London, 1971), pp. 28–33. R. V. Holdsworth, "*The Revenger's Tragedy*, Ben Jonson, and *The Devil's Law Case*," *Review of English Studies*, n.s. 31 (1980): 305–10, suggests that *The Revenger's Tragedy* may have influenced *Volpone*, rather than vice versa.

15. W. W. Greg, "Authorship Attributions in the Early Play-Lists, 1656–1671," *Edinburgh Bibliographical Society Transactions* 2 (1938–45): 305–29 (316–17).

16. *The Plays of Beaumont and Fletcher* (New Haven, Conn., 1927), p. 90.

17. G. E. Bentley, *The Jacobean and Caroline Stage* (Oxford, 1941–68), 3: 8.

18. Greg, "Early Play-Lists," p. 322.

19. Ibid., p. 318.

20. W. W. Greg, "Shakespeare and *Arden of Feversham*," *Review of English Studies* 21 (1945): 135.

21. David J. Lake, *The Canon of Thomas Middleton's Plays* (Cambridge, 1975), p. 140. Lake (pp. 140–42) cites three other examples, involving Lyly, Massinger, and Chapman.

22. David L. Frost, *The School of Shakespeare* (Cambridge, 1968), pp. 259–61. The matter is further discussed by MacD. P. Jackson, *Studies in Attribution: Middleton and Shakespeare* (Salzburg, 1979), pp. 170–73.

23. See G. E. Bentley, *The Profession of Dramatist in Shakespeare's Time* (Princeton, N. J., 1971), for the difference between "attached" and "unattached" playwrights. The quotation concerning Middleton is from p. 35. Evidence for an early connection between Middleton and the King's Men is summarized in Jackson, *Studies in Attribution*, pp. 174–76. For Middleton's early excursions into tragedy see Bentley, *The Jacobean and Caroline Stage*, 4: 855–911, and R. H. Barker, *Thomas Middleton* (New York, 1958), pp. 9–13.

24. E. K. Chambers, *The Elizabethan Stage* (Oxford, 1923), 3: 500, and 4:

126–27. The title page of *The Atheist's Tragedy* (1611) informs us that "in diuers places it hath often beene Acted," but it is doubtful whether the publisher would have been content with this rather lame inducement to prospective buyers had the play been performed by a prestigious company at a well-known theater. In June 1613 the dramatist Robert Daborne informed Philip Henslowe that he had assigned Tourneur the writing of one act of his play (now lost) called *The Arraignment of London* (Greg, ed., *Henslowe Papers* [London, 1907], pp. 72, 75). So Tourneur was probably prepared to sell his work to any company. For the date of composition of *The Atheist's Tragedy* see Irving Ribner's Revels edition of the play (London, 1964), pp. xxiii–xxv.

25. The few scraps of objective evidence put forward in support of Tourneur's authorship have been demonstrated to be worthless. David J. Lake, "*The Revenger's Tragedy:* Internal Evidence for Tourneur's Authorship Negated," *Notes and Queries* 216 (1971): 455–56.

26. "On the Authorship of *The Revenger's Tragedy,*" *English Studies* 41 (1960): 225–40. The phrase *as entities* is hers. Among critics who have sensed a continuity between *The Revenger's Tragedy* and *The Atheist's Tragedy* are: Harold Jenkins, "Cyril Tourneur," *Review of English Studies* 17 (1941): 21–36; H. H. Adams, "Cyril Tourneur on Revenge," *Journal of English and Germanic Philology* 48 (1949): 72–87; Robert Ornstein, "The Ethical Design of *The Revenger's Tragedy,*" *English Literary History* 21 (1954): 81–93, and *The Moral Vision of Jacobean Tragedy* (Madison, Wis., 1960), pp. 105–27; John D. Peter, "*The Revenger's Tragedy* Reconsidered," *Essays in Criticism* 6 (1956): 131–42, and *Complaint and Satire in Early English Literature* (Oxford, 1956), pp. 255–87; Irving Ribner, *Jacobean Tragedy: The Quest for Moral Order* (London, 1962), pp. 72–96. Common to most of these studies is a tendency to exaggerate the moral orthodoxy of the play at the expense of its aggression, prurience, and élan. For fuller information see the surveys listed in n. 3 above.

27. E. H. C. Oliphant, ed., *Shakespeare and his Fellow Dramatists* (New York, 1929), 2: 93–94.

28. These influences are fully explored by Frost, *The School of Shakespeare,* pp. 23–76.

29. "On the Authorship of *The Revenger's Tragedy,*" p. 240.

30. Barker in *Thomas Middleton* assumed Middleton's authorship of *The Revenger's Tragedy,* and Samuel Schoenbaum included a chapter on the play in *Middleton's Tragedies: A Critical Study* (New York, 1955). Such contributors to the authorship debate as Oliphant, Dunkel, Power, Mincoff, Price, Barber, Frost, and Lake (to whose work full references are given in other notes or in the surveys listed in n. 3) have all taken a "specialist" interest in Middleton.

31. Felix E. Schelling, *Elizabethan Drama, 1558–1642* (New York, 1908), 1: 568; David M. Holmes, *The Art of Thomas Middleton* (Oxford, 1970). Samuel Schoenbaum circumspectly maintained the compatibility of "*The Revenger's Tragedy* and Middleton's Moral Outlook," *Notes and Queries* 196 (1951): 8–10, but later, in *Internal Evidence and Elizabethan Dramatic Authorship* (Evanston, Ill., 1966), pp. 213–14, conceded a distinction between "moral outlook" and "moral passion."

32. *Jacobean Tragedy,* p. 86.

33. W. T. Jewkes, "The Nightmares of Internal Evidence in Jacobean Drama," *Seventeenth-Century News* 24 (1966): 4–8; this and the next two quotations are from p. 8.

34. This defect also vitiates studies of imagery. Una Ellis-Fermor and Marco Mincoff, independently investigating imagery, came to opposite conclusions, in "The Imagery of *The Revenger's Tragedie* and *The Atheist's Tragedie*," *Modern Language Review* 30 (1935): 289–301, and "The Authorship of *The Revenger's Tragedy*," *Studia Historico-Philologica Serdicensia* 2 (1940): 1–87, respectively. It remains true that Ellis-Fermor's article is perfunctory and ill-considered, finding resemblances between *The Revenger's Tragedy* and *The Atheist's Tragedy* without even using a Middleton play as control, whereas Mincoff's is a substantial contribution to criticism. But two later critics have again drawn opposite conclusions from their study of imagery, Inga-Stina Ekeblad, "An Approach to Tourneur's Imagery," *Modern Language Review* 54 (1959): 489–98, arguing for Tourneur, and Sanford Sternlicht, "Tourneur's Imagery and *The Revenger's Tragedy*," *Papers on Language and Literature* 6 (1970): 192–97, for Middleton.

35. *Middleton's Tragedies,* pp. 153–82.

36. Peter B. Murray, "The Authorship of *The Revenger's Tragedy*," *PBSA* 56 (1962): 195–218; incorporated in his book, *A Study of Cyril Tourneur* (Philadelphia, 1964); Cyrus Hoy, "The Shares of Fletcher and his Collaborators in the Beaumont and Fletcher Canon," *Studies in Bibliography* 8 (1956)–15 (1962).

37. *Cyril Tourneur,* pp. 165–66.

38. Review of *Cyril Tourneur, Notes and Queries* 212 (1967): 233–37.

39. Proudfoot's arguments, accepted uncritically by Charles Forker in his useful summary (p. 269) mentioned in n. 3 above, are countered in my *Studies in Attribution*, pp. 34–39.

40. *Cyril Tourneur,* p. 173.

41. See my "Compositorial Practices in Tourneur's *The Atheist's Tragedy*," *Studies in Bibliography* 32 (1979): 210–15, and "Compositorial Practices in *The Revenger's Tragedy*, 1607–08," *PBSA* 75 (1981): 157–70.

42. David J. Lake, *the Canon of Thomas Middleton's Plays* (Cambridge, 1975); MacD. P. Jackson, *Studies in Attribution: Middleton and Shakespeare* (Salzburg, 1979). About half the plays in each control corpus were absent from the other, and Hoy also offered linguistic data for well over a hundred early seventeenth-century plays, several of which were ignored by Lake and myself. Lake states specifically that in selecting his control corpus he read "every play written for the London commercial stages by known authors within the period 1600–1627: the authors excluded are those whose linguistic styles are very different from those of the problem plays" (p. 19). I read or at least checked all but a handful of unobtainable plays recorded in the Schoenbaum-Harbage *Annals of English Drama* as written between 1590 and 1630, and read or glanced through most plays fifteen years either side of that range.

43. *Studies in Attribution,* pp. 185–88; see also pp. 34–35.

44. George R. Price, "The Authorship and the Bibliography of *The Revenger's Tragedy*," *The Library*, 5th ser., 15 (1960): 262–77; Jackson, "Compositorial Practices in *The Revenger's Tragedy*, 1607–08," pp. 168–69.

45. There is a fuller discussion of this link between the *Revenger's Tragedy* quarto and Middleton in my "Compositorial Practices in *The Revenger's Tragedy* 1607–08," pp. 169–70. R. C. Bald, ed., *A Game at Chesse* (Cambridge, 1929).

46. Review of *The Canon of Thomas Middleton's Plays, Modern Language Review* 72 (1977): 897.

47. These points are developed more fully in *Studies in Attribution,* pp. 23–26, 35.

48. *Studies in Attribution,* pp. 67–79, 190–201.

49. Ibid., pp. 80–93, 202–07. A revised and expanded version of my chapter on function words is forthcoming in *Computers and the Humanities* as "Function Words, Style, and Authorship in English Renaissance Drama: The Case of *The Revenger's Tragedy.*" For the use of function words in authorship problems see Frederick Mosteller and David L. Wallace, *Inference and Disputed Authorship: The Federalist* (Reading, Mass., 1964), and A. Q. Morton, *Literary Detection: How to Prove Authorship and Fraud in Literature and Documents* (London, 1978).

50. The fullest treatment of this subject is by Lake, *The Canon of Thomas Middleton's Plays,* pp. 257–69. Metrical data were offered by R. H. Barker, "The Authorship of *The Second Maiden's Tragedy* and *The Revenger's Tragedy,*" *Shakespeare Association Bulletin* 20 (1945): 127; and Fred L. Jones, "Cyril Tourneur," *Times Literary Supplement,* 18 June 1931, p. 487, and "An Experiment with Massinger's Verse," *PMLA* 47 (1932): 727–40. See also *Studies in Attribution,* pp. 162–64, 208.

51. *The Canon of Thomas Middleton's Plays,* p. 265.

52. *Pause Patterns in Elizabethan and Jacobean Drama* (Gainesville, Fla., 1960).

53. Ibid., p. 2.

54. Ibid., pp. 28–31.

55. Besides *A Trick,* the Middleton plays are *Hengist, No Wit, No Help Like a Woman's,* and *The Phoenix.* Shirley is the only other dramatist with more than a single play among the top dozen matchings: he has two, *The Traitor* and *Hyde Park,* both of which belong to the 1630s, a quarter of a century after *The Revenger's Tragedy* was composed. Shirley's verse is in most respects totally unlike the verse of *The Revenger's Tragedy;* indeed, in its extravagant use of the run-on line it closely resembles Tourneur's.

56. The affirmative "Ay" prevails in *The Revenger's Tragedy* and in Middleton's early plays, whereas Tourneur in *The Atheist's Tragedy* prefers the more fashionable "Yes." MacD. P. Jackson, "Affirmative Particles in *Henry VIII,*" *Notes and Queries* 207 (1962): 372–74. This type of evidence has been thoroughly explored by Lake. The quarto is like Middleton's plays in its unusual freedom from parentheses (*Studies in Attribution,* pp. 96–99, 124–31). This is a trivial point, but such evidence is helpful in confirming otherwise established divisions in Middleton-Rowley and Middleton-Dekker plays. Most important, Lake has made the necessary negative check of certain words, phrases, and parallels cited by earlier scholars in support of Middleton's claims. He finds that many of these are genuinely distinctive (pp. 143–49). The remarkably exact and extensive verbal parallel that Barker (*Thomas Middleton,* pp. 70–71) noted between *The Revenger's Tragedy,* IV.ii, and Middleton's *A Mad World My Masters,* III.iii, implies either plagiarism or common authorship.

57. *The Works of Cyril Tourneur,* p. 21.

58. Both phrases are by R. A. Foakes, "On the Authorship of *The Revenger's Tragedy,*" *Modern Language Review* 48 (1953): 138.

59. Russell A. Fraser and Norman Rabkin, ed., *Drama of the English Renaissance* (New York, 1976), 2: 21.

60. H. J. Eysenck and D. K. B. Nias, *Sex, Violence and the Media* (London, 1978), p. 28.

61. Foakes, Review of *The Canon of Thomas Middleton's Plays, Modern Language Review* 72 (1977): 896. For instance, it is true that scribes, compositors, and even authors themselves in copying their own work may alter spellings and linguistic forms; that expletives were subject to censorship, besides varying with genre; that function-word rates achieve only partial separation between Middleton and non-Middleton plays; and that editorial rearrangement of verse may affect line endings (though not pause patterns of the split-line type). These problems are discussed, in general and in particular cases, in both Lake, *The Canon of Thomas Middleton's Plays* and Jackson, *Studies in Attribution*.

The Revenger's Tragedy (Facsimile)

THE
REVENGERS
TRAGÆDIE.

As it hath beene sundry times Acted,
by the Kings Maiesties
Seruants.

AT LONDON
Printed by G. E l d, and are to be sold at his
house in Fleete-lane at the signe of the
Printers-Presse.
1 6 0 8.

The Reuengers Tragædie.

Enter Vendici, *the Duke,* Dutcheſſe, Luſurioſo *her ſonne,*
Spurio *the baſtard, with a traine. paſſe ouer the*
Stage with Torch-light.

Vindi. DVke: royall letchr ; goe, gray hayrde adultery,
And thou his ſonne, as impious ſteept as hee :
And thou his baſtard true-begott in euill :
And thou his Dutcheſſe that will doe with Diuill,
Foure exlent Characters---O that marrow-leſſe age,
Would ſtuffe the hollow Bones with dambd deſires,
And ſtead of heate kindle infernall fires,
Within the ſpend-thrift veynes of a drye **Duke,**
A parcht and iuiceleſſe luxur, O God ! one
That has ſcarce bloud inough to liue vpon.
And hee to ryot it like a ſonne and heyre ?
O the thought of that
Turnes my abuſed heart-ſtrings into fret.
Thou ſallow picture of my poyſoned loue,
My ſtudies ornament, thou ſhell of Death,
Once the bright face of my betrothed Lady,
When life and beauty naturally fild out
Theſe ragged impeifections ;
When two-heauen pointed Diamonds were ſet
In thoſe vnſightly Rings ; -- then 'twas a face
So farre beyond the artificiall ſhine
Of any womans bought complexion
That the vprighteſt man, (if ſuch there be,
That ſinne but ſeauen times a day) broke cuſtome
And made vp eight with looking after her,
Oh ſhe was able to ha made a Vſurers ſonne
Melt all his patrimony in a kiſſe,
And what his father fiftie yeares told
To haue conſumde, and yet his ſute beene cold :
But oh accurſed Pallace !
Thee when thou wert appareld in thy fleſh,
The old Duke poyſon'd,
Becauſe thy purer part would not conſent

Vnto

Vnto his palfey-luſt,for old men luſt-full
Do ſhow like young men angry, eager violent,
Out-bid like their limited performances
O ware an old man hot,and vicious
,, Age as in gold in luſt is couetous.
Vengence thou murders Quit-rent,and whereby
Thou ſhoulſt thy ſelfe Tennant to Tragedy,
Oh keepe thy day,houre,minute, I beſeech,
For thoſe thou haſt determind:hum:who ere knew
Murder vnpayd,faith giue Reuenge her due
Sha's kept touch hetherto—be merry,merry,
Aduance thee,O thou terror to fat folkes
To haue their coſtly three-pilde fleſh worne of
As bare as this---for banquets:eaſe and laughter,
Can make great men as greatneſſe goes by clay,
But wiſe men little are more great then they?

Enter her brother Hippolito.

Hip. Still ſighing ore deaths vizard.
   Vind. Brother welcome,
What comfort bringſt thou?how go things at **Court?**
   Hip. In ſilke and ſiluer brother:neuer brauer.
   Vind. Puh,
Thou playſt vpon my meaning,pree-thee ſay
Has that bald Madam,Opportunity?
Yet thought vpon's, ſpeake are we happy yet?
Thy wrongs and mine are for one ſcabberd fit.
   Hip. It may proue happineſſe?
   Vind. What ill may proue?
Giue me to taſt.
   Hip. Giue me your hearing then,
You know my place at Court.
   Vind. I;the Dukes Chamber
But tis a maruaile thourt not turnd out yet!
   Hip. Faith I haue beene ſhooud at,but twas ſtill my hap
To hold by'th Ducheſſe skirt,you geſſe at that,
Whome ſuch a Coate keepes vp can nere fall flat,
But to the purpoſe.
Laſt euening predeceſſor vnto this,

The

The Dukes ſonne warily enquird for me,
Whoſe pleaſure I attended: he began,
By policy to open and vnhuſke me
About the time and common rumour :
But I had ſo much wit to keepe my thoughts
Vp in their built houſes, yet afforded him
An idle ſatifaction without danger,
But the whole ayme, and ſcope of his intent
Ended in this, coniuring me in priuate,
To ſeeke ſome ſtrange digeſted fellow forth:
Of ill-contented nature, either diſgracſt
In former times, or by new groomes diſplacſt,
Since his Step-mothers nuptialls, ſuch a bloud
A man that were for euill onely good;
To giue you the true word ſome baſe coynd Pander?

   Vind. I reach you, for I know his heate is ſuch,
Were there as many Concubines as Ladies
He would not be contaynd, he muſt flie out:
I wonder how ill featurde, vilde proportiond
That one ſhould be : if ſhe were made for woman,
Whom at the Inſurrection of his luſt
He would refuſe for once, heart, I thinke none,
Next to a ſkull, tho more vnſound then one
Each face he meetes he ſtrongly doates vpon.

   Hip. Brother y'aue truly ſpoke him?
He knowes not you, but Ile ſweare you know him.

   Vind. And therefore ile put on that knaue for once,
And be a right man then, a man a'th Time,
For to be honeſt is not to be ith world,
Brother ile be that ſtrange compoſed fellow.

   Hip. And ile prefer you brother.

   Vind. Go too then,
The ſmallſt aduantage fattens wronged men
It may point out, occaſion, if I meete her,
Ile hold her by the fore-top faſt ynough;
Or like the *French Moale* heaue vp hayre and all,
I haue a habit that wil fit it quaintly,
Here comes our Mother.   *Hip.* And ſiſter.

           Vind.

Vind. We must quoyne.
Women are apt you know to take falſe money,
But I dare ſtake my ſoule for theſe two creatures
Onely excuſe excepted that they'le ſwallow,
Becauſe their ſexe is eaſie in beleefe.

Moth. What newes from Cour ſonne *Carlo?*

Hip. Faith Mother,
Tis whiſperd there the Ducheſſe yongeſt ſonne
Has playd a Rape on Lord *Antonios* wife.

Moth. On that relligious Lady!

Caſt. Royall bloud:monſter he deſerues to die,
If *Italy* had no more hopes but he.

Vin. Siſter y'aue ſentenc'd moſt direct, and true,
The Lawes a woman, and would ſhe were you:
Mother I muſt take leaue of you.

Moth. Leaue for what?

Vin. I intend ſpeedy trauaile.

Hip. That he do's Madam.   *Mo.* Speedy indeed!

Vind. For ſince my worthy fathers funerall,
My life's vnnaturally to me, e'en compeld
As if I liu'd now when I ſhould be dead.

Mot. Indeed he was a worthy Gentleman
Had his eſtate beene fellow to his mind.

Vind. The Duke did much deiect him.

Moth. Much?

Vind. To much.
And through diſgrace oft ſmotherd in his ſpirit,
When it would mount, ſurely I thinke hee dyed
Of diſcontent:the Noblemans conſumption.

Moth. Moſt ſure he did!

Vind. Did he? lack,——you know all
You were his mid-night ſecretary.

Moth. No.
He was to wiſe to truſt me with his thoughts.

Vind. Yfaith then father thou waſt wiſe indeed,
,, Wiues are but made to go to bed and feede.
Come mother, ſiſter :youle bring me onward brother?

Hip. I will.

Vind.

Vind. Ile quickly turne into another.   *Exeunt.*

Enter the old Duke, Luſurioſo *, his ſonne,the Ducheſſe : the Baſt-
ard, the Ducheſſe two ſonnes* Ambitioſo *, and* Superuacuo *,the
third her yongeſt brought out with Officers for the Rape two
Iudges.*

Duke. Ducheſſe it is your yongeſt ſonne,we're ſory,
His violent Act has e'en drawne bloud of honor
And ſtaind our honors,
Throwne inck vpon the for-head of our ſtate
Which eruious ſpirits will dip their pens into
After our death;and blot vs in our Toombes.
For that which would ſeeme treaſon in our liues
Is laughter when we're dead,who dares now whiſper
That dares not then ſpeake out, and e'en proclaime,
With lowd words and broad pens our cloſeſt ſhame.

Iut. Your grace hath ſpoke like to your ſiluer yeares
Full of confirmed grauity; — for what is it to haue,
A flattering falſe inſculption on a Toombe:
And in mens hearts reproch,the boweld Corps,
May be ſeard in,but with free tongue I ſpeake,
„ The faults of great men through their ſearce **clothes breake.**

Duk. They do , we're ſory for't,it is our fate,
To liue in feare and die to liue in hate,
I leaue him to your ſentance dome him **Lords**
The fact is great;whilſt I ſit by and ſigh.

*Duch.*My gratious Lord I pray be mercifull,
Although his treſpaſſe far exceed his yeares,
Thinke him to be your owne as I am yours,
Call him not ſonne in law:the law I feare
Wil fal too ſoone vpon his name and him:
Temper his fault with pitty?

Luſſ. Good my Lord.
Then twill not taſt ſo bitter and vnpleaſant
Vpon the Iudges pallat,for offences
Gilt ore with mercy,ſhow like fayreſt women,
Good onely for therr beauties , which waſht of: no ſin is oug-
    Ambitiſ I beſeech your grace,   (lier
Be ſoft and mild,let not *Relentleſſe* **Law,**

                    Looke

Looke with an iron for-head on our brother,

    Spu He yeelds small comfort yet, hope he shall die,
And if a bastards wish might stand in force,
Would all the court were turnde into a coarse,

    Duc, No pitty yet ? must I rise fruitlesse then,
A wonder in a woman; are my knees,
Of such lowe--mettall-- that without Respect----

    1.*iudg.* Let the offender stand forth,
Tis the Dukes pleasure that Impartiall Doome,
Shall take first hold of his vncleane attempt,
A Rape ! why tis the very core of lust,
Double Adultery.

    Iuni. So Sir.

    2.*Iud.* And which was worse,
Committed on the Lord *Antonioes* wife,
That Generall honest Lady, confesse my Lord!
What mou'd you toot?

    Iuni. why flesh and blood my Lord.
What should moue men vnto a woman else,

    Luss. O do not iest thy doome, trust not an axe
Or sword too far; the Law is a wise serpent
And quickly can beguile thee of thy life,
Tho marriage onely has mad thee my brother,
I loue thee so far, play not with thy Death,

    Iuni. I thanke you troth, good admonitions faith,
If ide the grace now to make vse of them,

    1.*Iud.* That Ladyes name has spred such a faire wing
Ouer all *Italy*; that if our Tongs,
Were sparing toward the Fact, Iudgment it selfe,
Would be condemned and suffer in mens thoughts,

    Iuni. Well then tis done, and it would please me well
Were it to doe agen: sure snees a Goddesse,
For ide no power to see her, and to liue,
It falls out true in this for I must die,
Her beauty was ordaynd to be my scaffold,
And yet my thinks I might be easier ceast,
My fault being sport, let me but die in iest,

    1.*Iud.* This be the sentence,

Duc.

Dut. O keepe vpon your Tongue,let it not flip,
Death too foone fteales out of a Lawyers lip,
Be not fo crueil-wife?
   1.*Iudg.* Your Grace muft pardon vs,
'Tis but the Iuftice of the Lawe.
   Dut. The Lawe,
Is growne more fubtill then a woman fhould be.
   Spu. Now,now he dyes,rid 'em away.
   Dut. O what it is to haue an old-coole Duke,
To bee as flack in tongue,as in performance.
   1.*Iudr.* Confirmde, this be the doome irreuocable.
   Dut. Oh!   1.*Iudg.* To morrow early.
   Dut. Pray be a bed my Lord.
   1.*Iudr.* Your Grace much wrongs your felfe.
   Ambi. No'tis that tongue,
Your too much right,dos do vs too much wrong.
   1.*Iudg.* Let that offender ————
   Dut. Liue and be in health.
   1.*Iud* Be on a Scaffold---*Duk.*Hold,hold,my Lord.
   Spu. Pax ont,
What makes my Dad fpeake now?
   Duke. We will defer the iudgement till next fitting,
In the meane time let him be kept clofe prifoner:
Guard beare him hence.
   Ambi. Brother,this makes for thee,
Feare not, weele haue a trick to fet thee free.
   *Iuni.*Brother,I will expect it from you both; and in that hope
I reft.   *Super.* Farewell,be merry.   *Exit with a garde.*
   Spu. Delayd, deferd nay then if iudgement haue cold bloud,
Flattery and bribes will kill it.
   Duke. About it then my Lords with your beft powers,
More ferious bufineffe calls vpon our houres. *Exe.manet Du.*
   Dut. Waft euer knowne ftep-Dutcheffe was fo milde,
And calme as I? fome now would plot his death,
With eafie Doctors,thofe loofe liuing men,
And make his witherd Grace fall to his Graue,
And keepe Church better?
Some fecond wife would do this,and difpatch

B   Her

Her double loathd Lord at meate and sleepe,
Indeed 'tis true an old mans twice a childe,
Mine cannot speake, one of his single words,
Would quite haue free d my yongeſt decreſt ſonne
From death or durance, and haue made him walke
With a bold foote vpon the thornie law,
Whoſe Prickles ſhould bow vnder hi n, but 'tis not,
And therefore wedlock faith ſhall be forgot,
Ile kill him in his fore-head, hate there feede,
That wound is deepeſt tho it neuer bleed :
And here comes hee whom my heart points vnto,
His baſtard ſonne, but my loues true-begot,
Many a wealthy letter haue I ſent him,
Sweld vp with Iewels, and the timorous man
Is yet but coldly kinde,
That Iewel's mine that quiuers in his eare,
Mocking his Maiſters chilneſſe and vaine feare,
Ha's ſpide me now.

    Spu. Madame ? your Grace ſo priuate.
My duety on your hand.

    Dut. Vpon my hand ſir, troth I thinke youde feare,
To kiſſe my hand too if my lip ſtood there,

    Spi. Witneſſe I would not Madam.

    Dut. Tis a wonder,
For ceremonie ha's made many fooles,
It is as eaſie way vnto a Dutcheſſe,
As to a Hatted-dame, (if her loue anſwer)
But that by timorous honors, pale reſpects,
Idle degrees of feare, men make their wayes
Hard of themſelues——what haue you thought of me?

    Spi. Madam I euer thinke of you, in duty,
Regard and ————

    Dut. Puh, vpon my loue I meane.

    Spu. I would 'twere loue, but 'tus a fowler name
Then luſt ; you are my fathers wife, your Grace may geſſe now,
What I could call it.

    Dut. Why th'art his ſonne but falſly, ꞌ
Tis a hard queſtion whether he begot thee.

                                   Spu.

Spu. Ifaith 'tis true too ; Ime an vncertaine man,
Of more vncertaine woman ; may be his groome 'ath ſtable be-
got me, you know I know not, hee could ride a horſe well, a
ſhrowd ſuſpition marry--- hee was wondrous tall, hee had his
length yfaith, for peeping ouer halfe ſhut holy-day windowes,
Men would deſire him light, when he was a foote,
He made a goodly ſhow vnder a Pent-houſe,
And when he rid, his Hatt would check the ſignes, and clatter
Barbers Baſons.

Dut. Nay ſet you a horſe back once,
Youle nere light off.

Spu. Indeed I am a beggar.

Dut. That's more the ſigne thou'art Great---but to our loue.
Let it ſtand firme both in thought and minde,
That the Duke was thy father, as no doubt then
Hee bid faire fort, thy iniurie is the more,
For had hee cut thee a right Diamond,
Thou hadſt beene next ſet in the Duke-doomes Ring,
When his worne ſelfe like Ages eaſie ſlaue,
Had dropt out of the Collet into th' Graue,
What wrong can equall this? canſt thou be tame
And thinke vppon't.

Spu. No mad and thinke vpon't.

Dut. Who would not be reuengd of ſuch a father,
E'en in the worſt way? I would thanke that ſinne,
That could moſt iniury him, and bee in league with it,
Oh what a griefe 'tis, that a man ſhould liue
But once ith world, and then to liue a Baſtard,
The curſe a'the wombe, the theefe of Nature,
Begot againſt the ſeauenth commandement,
Halfe dambd in the conception, by the iuſtice
Of that vnbribed euerlaſting law.

Spu. Oh Ide a hot-backt Diuill to my father.

Dut. Would not this mad e'en patience, make bloud rough?
Who but an Eunuch would not ſinne? his bed
By one falſe minute diſinherited.

Spi. I, there's the vengeance that my birth was wrapt in,
Ile be reuengd for all, now hate begin,

Ile

Ile call soule Inceſt but a Veniall ſinne.

Dut. Cold ſtill:in vaine then muſt a Dutcheſſe woo ?

Spu. Madam I bluſh to ſay what I will doo.

Dut. Thence flew ſweet comfort, earneſt and farewell.

Spu. Oh one inceſtuous kiſſe picks open hell.

Dut. Faith now old Duke; my vengeance ſhall reach high,

Ile arme thy brow with womans Herauldrie.   *Exit.*

Spu Duke,thou didſt do me wrong,and by thy Act

Adultery is my nature ;

Faith if the truth were knowne,I was begot

After ſome gluttonous dinner,ſome ſtirring diſh

Was my firſt father ; when deepe healths went round,

And Ladies cheekes were painted red with Wine,

Their tongues as ſhort and nimble as their heeles

Vttering words ſweet and thick ; and when they riſe,

Were merrily diſpoſd to fall agen,

In ſuch a whiſpring and with-drawing houre,

When baſe-male-Bawds kept Centinell at ſtaire-head

Was I ſtolne ſoftly ; oh---damnation met

The ſinne of feaſts,drunken adultery.

I feele it ſwell me ; my reuenge is iuſt,

I was begot in impudent Wine and Luſt :

Step-mother I conſent to thy deſires,

I loue thy miſchiefe well,but I hate thee,

And thoſe three Cubs thy ſonnes,wiſhing confuſion

Death and diſgrace may be their Epitaphs,

As for my brother the Dukes onely ſonne,

Whoſe birth is more beholding to report

Then mine,and yet perhaps as falſely ſowne.

(Women muſt not be truſted with their owne)

Ile looſe my dayes vpon him hate all I,

Duke on thy browe Ile drawe my Baſtardie.

For indeed a baſtard by nature ſhould make Cuckolds,

Becauſe he is the ſonne of a Cuckold-maker.   *Exit.*

     Enter Vindici *and* Hippolito, Vindici *in diſguiſe to*

        attend L. Luſſurioſo *the Dukes ſonne.*

    Vind What brother ? am I farre inough from my ſelfe?

Hip. As if another man had beene ſent whole

Into the world, and none wift how he came.

Vind. It wil confirme me bould: the child a'th **Court**,
Let blufhes dwell i'th Country. impudence!
Thou Goddeffe of the pallace, Miftrs of Mifteffes
To whom the coftly perfumd-people pray,
Strike thou my fore-head into dauntleffe Marble;
Mine eyes to fteady Saphires: turne my vifage,
And if I muft needes glow, let me blufh inward
That this immodeft feafon may not fpy,
That fcholler in my cheekes, foole-bafhfullnes.
That Maide in the old time, whofe flufh of *Grace*
Would neuer fuffer her to get good cloaths;
Our maides are wifer; and are leffe afhamd,
Saue *Grace* the bawde I feldome heare *Grace* nam'd!

Hip. Nay brother you reach out a'th Verge now, -- Sfoote
the Dukes fonne, fettle your lookes.

    Vind. Pray let me not be doubted.   *Hip.* My Lord---

    Luff. Hipolito?--be abfent leaue vs.

Hip. My Lord after long fearch, wary inquiryes
And politick fiftings, I made choife of yon fellow,
Whom I geffe rare for many deepe imployments;
This our age fwims within him: and if Time
Had fo much hayre, I fhould take him for Time,
He is fo neere kinne to this prefent minute?

    Luff. Tis ynough.
We thanke thee: yet words are but great-mens blanckes
Gold tho it be dum do's vtter the beft thankes.

Hip. Your plenteous honor---an exlent fellow my Lord.

Luff. So, giue vs leaue--welcome, bee not far off, we muft bee
better acquainted, pufh, be bould with vs, thy hand:

Vind. With all my heart yfaith how doft fweete Muf k-cat
When fhall we lie togither?

    Luff. Wondrous knaue!
Gather him into bouldneffe, Sfoote the flaue's
Already as familiar as an Ague,
And fhakes me at his pleafure, friend I can
Forget my felfe in priuate, but elfe where,
J pray do you remember me.

        Vind.

Vind. Oh very well sir——I conster my selfe sawcy!

Luss. What hast beene,
Of what profession.

Vind. A bone-setter!   *Luss.* A bone-setter!

Vind. A bawde my Lord,
One that setts bones togither.

Luss. Notable bluntnesse?
Fit, sit for me, e'en traynd vp to my hand
Thou hast beene Scriuener to much knauery then.

Vind. Foole, to abundance sir; I haue beene witnesse
To the surrenders of a thousand virgins,
And not so little,
I haue seene Patrimonyes washt a peices
Fruit-feilds turnd into bastards,
And in a world of Acres,
Not so much dust due to the heire t'was left too
As would well grauell a petition'

Luss. Fine villaine? troth I like him wonderously
Hees e'en shapt for my purpose, then thou knowst
Ith world strange lust.

Vind. O Dutch lust! fulsome lust!
Druncken procrearion, which begets, so many drunckards;
Some father dreads not (gonne to bedde in wine) to slide from
the mother,
And cling the daughter-in-law,
Some Vncles are adulterous with their Neeces,
Brothers with brothers wiues, O howre of Incest!
Any kin now next to the Rim ath sister
Is mans meate in these dayes, and in the morning
When they are vp and drest, and their maske on,
Who can perceiue this? saue that eternall eye
That see's through flesh and all, well:--If any thing be dambd?
It will be twelue a clock at night; that twelue
Will neuer scape;
It is the *Iudas* of the howers; wherein,
Honest saluation is betrayde to sin,

Luss. Introth it is too? but let this talke glide
It is our bloud to erre, tho hell gapte lowde

Ladies

Ladies know *Lucifer* fell, yet ftill are proude!
Now fir? wert thou as fecret as thou'rt fubtil,
And deepely fadomd into all eftates
I would embrace thee for a neere imployment,
And thou fhouldft fwell in money, and be able.
To make lame beggers crouch to thee.

    Vind. My Lord?
Secret? I nere had that difeafe ath mother
I praife my father: why are men made cloffe?
But to keepe thoughts in beft , I grant you this
Tell but fome woman a fecret ouer night,
Your doctor may finde it in the vrinall ith morning,
But my Lord.

    Luff. So, thou'rt confirmd in mee
And thus I enter thee.

    Vind. This Indian diuill,
Will quickly enter any man : but a Vfurer,
He preuents that, by entring the diuill firft.

    Luff. Attend me. I am paft my depht in luft
And I muft fwim or drowne, all my defires
Are leueld at a Virgin not far from Court,
To whom I haue conuayde by Meffenger
Many waxt Lines, full of my neateft fpirit,
And iewells that were able to rauifh her
Without the helpe of man; all which and more
Shee foolifh chaft fent back , the meffengers,
Receiuing frownes for anfweres.

    Vind. Poffible!
Tis a rare *Phænix* who ere fhe bee,
If your defires be fuch, fhe fo repugnant,
In troth my Lord ide be reuengde and marry her.

    Lufs. Pufh; the doury of her bloud & of her fortunes,
Are both too meane,--good ynough to be bad withal
Ime one of that number can defend
Marriage is good: yet rather keepe a friend,
Giue me my bed by ftealth--theres true delight
What breeds a loathing in't, but night by night.

    Vind. A very fine relligion?

                                     Lufs.

Luſſ. Therefore thus,
He truſt thee in the buſineſſe of my heart
Becauſe I ſee thee wel experienc'ſt
In this Luxurious day wherein we breath,
Go thou, and with a ſmooth enchaunting tongue
Bewitch her eares, and Couzen her of all Grace
Enter vpon the portion of her ſoule,
Her honor, which ſhe calls her chaſtity
And bring it into expence, for honeſty
Is like a ſtock of money layd to ſleepe,
Which nere ſo little broke, do's neuer keep:
　Vind. You haue giut the Tang yſaith my Lord
Make knowne the Lady to me, and my braine,
Shall ſwell with ſtrange Inuention: I will moue it
Till I expire with ſpeaking, and drop downe
Without a word to ſaue me; ---but ile worke ―――――
　Luſſ. We thanke thee, and will raiſe thee :--receiue her name,
it is the only daughter, to Madame *Gratiana* the late widdow
　Vind. Oh, my ſiſter, my ſiſter?-- *Luſſ.* Why doſt walke aſide?
　Vind. My Lord, I was thinking how I might begin
As thus, oh Ladie—or twenty hundred deuices,
Her very bodkin will put a man in,
　Luſſ. Lor the wagging of her haire.
　Vind. No, that ſhall put you in my Lord.
　Luſſ. Shal't? why content, doſt know the daughter then?
　Vind. O exlent well by ſight,
　Luſſ. That was her brother
That did prefer thee to vs.
　Vind. My Lord I thinke ſo,
I knew I had ſcene him ſome where---
　Luſſ. And therefore pree-thee let thy heart to him,
Be as a Virgin, cloſſe. 　　　　*Vind.* Oh me good Lord.
　Luſſ. We may laugh at that ſimple age within him;
　Vind. Ha ha, ha.
　Luſſ. Himſelfe being made the ſubtill inſtrument,
To winde vp a good fellow,
　Vind. That's I my Lord.
　Luſſ. That's thou.

To entice and worke his sister.

   Vind. A pure nouice?   *Luss.* T'was finely manag'd.

   Vind. Gallantly carried;

A prety-perfumde villaine.

   Luss. I'ue bethought me

If she prooue chaft ftill and immoueable,

Venture vpon the Mother, and with giftes

As I will furnish thee, begin with her.

Vin. Oh fie, fie, that's the wrong end my Lord. Tis meere impof-

fible that a mother by any gifts should become a bawde to her

owne Daughter!

   Luss. Nay then I fee thou'rt but a puny in the fubtill Miftery of

a woman:--why tis held now no dainty dish: The name

Is fo in league with age, that now adaies

It do's Eclipfe three quarters of a Mother;

   Vind. Doft fo my Lord?

Let me alone then to Eclipfe the fourth.

   Luss. Why well fayd, come ile furnish thee, but firft

fweare to be true in all.

   Vind. True?   *Luss.* Nay but fweare!

   Vind. Sweare?--I hope your honor little doubts my fayth.

   Luss. Yet for my humours fake caufe I loue fwearing.

   Vind. Caufe you loue fwearing, flud I will.

   Luss. Why ynough,

Ere long looke to be made of better ftuff.

   Vind. That will do well indeed my Lord.

   Luss. Attend me?

   Vind. Oh.

Now let me burft, I'ue eaten Noble poyfon.

We are made ftrange fellowes, brother, innocent villaines,

Wilt not be angry when thou hearft on t, thinkft thou?

Ifayth thou shalt; fweate me to foule my fifter.

Sword I durft make a promife of him to thee,

Thou shalt dis-heire him, it shall be thine honor,

And yet now angry froath is downe in me,

It would not proue the meaneft policy

In this difguize to try the fayth of both,

Another might haue had the felfe fame office,

               C   Some

Some flaue,that would haue wrought effectually,
I and perhaps ore-wrought em,therefore I,
Being thought trauayld,will apply my felfe,
Vnto the felfe fame forme,forget my nature,
As if no part about me were kin to 'em,
So touch'em,----tho I durft almoft for good,
Venture my lands in heauen vpon their good.   *Exit.*

Enter the difcontented Lord Antonio , *whofe wife the Ducheffes*
      yongeft Sonne rauifht ; he Difcouering the body of her dead
      to certaine Lords : and Hippolito.

      L. *Ant.*Draw neerer Lords and be fad witneffes
Of a fayre comely building newly falne,
Being faifely vndermined:violent rape
Has playd a glorious act,behold my Lords
A fight that ftrikes man out of me:
      P.*ero.*That vertuous Lady?   *Ant.* Prefident for wiues?
      *Hip.*The blufh of many weomen,whofe chaft prefence,
Would ene call fhame vp to their cheekes,
And make pale wanton finners haue good colours.----
      L.*Ant.*Dead!
Her honor firft drunke poyfon,and her life,
Being fellowes in one houfe did pledge her honour,
      Pier.*O greefe of many!
      L *Anto.* I markt not this before.
A prayer Booke the pillow to her cheeke,
This was her rich confection, and another
Plafte'd in her right hand,with a leafe tuckt vp,
Poynting to thefe words.
      Melius virtute mori,Quam per Dedecus viuere.
True and effectuall it is indeed.
      *Hip.*My Lord fince you enuite vs to your forrowes,
Lets truely taft'em,that with equall comfort,
As to our felues we may releiue your wrongs,
We haue greefe too,that yet walkes without Tong,
      Cura leues loquuntur,Maiores ftupent.
      L.*Ant.*You deale with truth my Lord.
Lend me but your Attentions,and Ile cut
Long greefe into fhort words : laft reuelling night.

                                             When

When Torch-light made an artificiall noone
About the Court,fome Courtiers in the maske,
Putting on better faces then their owne,
Being full of frawde and flattery:amongft whome,
The Ducheſes yongeſt ſonne(that moth to honor)
Fild vp a Roome;and with long luſt to eat,
Into my wearing; amongſt all the Ladyes,
Singled out that deere forme;who euer liu'd,
As cold in Luſt;as ſhee is now in death;
(Which that ſtep Duches---Monſter knew to well;)
And therefore in the height of all the reuells,
When Muſick was hard lowdeſt,Courtiers buſieſt,
And Ladies great with laughter;---O Vitious minute!
Vnfit but for relation to be ſpoke of,
Then with a face more impudent then his vizard
He harried her amidſt a throng of Panders,
That liue vppon damnation of both kindes,
And fed the rauenous vulture of his luſt,
(O death to thinke ont)ſhe her honor forcſt,
Deemd it a nobler dowry for her name,
To die with poyſon then to liue with ſhame.
    Hip.A wondrous Lady;of rare fire compact,
Sh'as made her name an Empreſſe by that act,
     Pier.My Lord what iudgement followes the offender?
    L.Ant Faith none my Lord it cooles and is deferd,
     Pier.Delay the doome for rape?
     L.Ant,O you muſt note who tis ſhould die,
The Ducheſſe ſonne, ſheele looke to be a ſauer,
"Iudgment in this age is nere kin to fauour.
    Hip.Nay then ſtep forth thou *Bribeleſſe* officer;
I bind you all in ſteele to bind you ſurely,
Heer let your oths meet,to be kept and payd,
Which elſe will ſticke like ruſt,and ſhame the blade,
Strengthen my vow,that if at the next ſitting,
Iudgment ſpeake all in gold,and ſpare the bloud
Of ſuch a ſerpent,e'en before their ſeats,
To let his ſoule out,which long ſince was found,
Guilty in heauen.

                                                All.

*All.*We sweare it and will act it,

L. *Anto.*Kind Gentlemen,I thanke you in mine Ire,

*Hip.*Twere pitty?

The ruins of so faire a Monument,

Sould not be dipt in the defacers bloud,

*Piero.*Her funerall shall be wealthy,for her name,

Merits a toombe of pearle ; my Lord *Antonio*,

For this time wipe your Lady from your eyes,

No doubt our greefe and youres may one day court it,

When we are more familiar with Reueng,

L. *Anto.*That is my comfort Gentlemen, and I ioy,

In this one happines aboue the rest,

Which will be cald a miralce at last,

That being an old---man ide a wife so chast.   *Exeunt.*

ACTVS. 2. *SCÆ*. 1.
Enter Castiza *the sister.*

*Cast.*How hardly shall that mayden be beset,

Whose onely fortunes,are her constant thoughts,

That has no other childes-part but her honor,

That Keepes her lowe ; and empty in estate.

Maydes and their honors are like poore beginners,

Were not sinne rich there would be fewer sinners;

Why had not vertue a reuennewe ? well,

I know the cause,t wold haue impouerish'd hell.

How now *Dondolo*.

Don. *Madona*,there is one as they say a thing of flesh and blood,a man I take him by his beard that would very desire-ously mouth to mouth with you.

*Cast.*Whats that?

*Don.*Show his teeth in your company,

*Cast.*I vnderstand thee not;

*Don.*Why speake with you *Madona*!

Cast. Why say so mad-man ,and cut of a great deale of durty way ; had it not beene better spoke in ordinary words that one would speake with me.

*Don.*Ha,ha,thats as ordinary as two shillings,I would striue
alitle

alitle to show my selfe in my place, a Gentleman-vsher scornes
to vse the Phrase and fanzye of a seruingman.

 *Cast.*Yours be your one sir,go direct him hether,
I hope some happy tidings from my brother,
That lately trauayld,whome my soule affects.
Here he comes.

Enter Vindice *her brother disguised.*

 *Vin.*Lady the best of wishes to your sexe,
Faire skins and new gownes,

 *Cast.*Oh they shall thanke you sir,
Whence this,

 *Vin.*Oh from a deere and worthy friend,
mighty!   *Cast.*From whome?

 *Vin.*The Dukes sonne!

 *Cast.*Receiue that!

A boxe a:h eare to her Brother.

I swore I'de put anger in my hand,
And passe the Virgin limits of my selfe,
To him that next appear'd in that base office,
To be his sinnes Atturney,beare to him,
That figure of my hate vpon thy checke
Whilst tis yet hot, and Ile reward thee fort,
Tell him my honor shall haue a rich name,
When seuerall harlots shall share his with shame,
Farewell commend me to him in my hate!   *Exit.*

 *Vin.*It is the sweetest Boxe,
That ere my nose came nye,
The finest drawne-worke cuffe that ere was worne,
Ile loue this blowe for euer,and this cheeke
Shall still hence forward take the wall of this,
Oh Ime a boue my tong:most constant sister,
In this thou hast right honorable showne,
Many are cald by their honour that haue none,
Thou art approu'd for euer in my thoughts.
It is not in the power of words to raynt thee,
And yet for the saluation of my oth,
As my resolue in that poynt;I will lay,
Hard seige vnto my Mother,tho I know,

A Syrens.

A *Syrens* tongue could not bewitch her so.
Masse fitly here she comes, thankes my disguize,
Madame good afternoone.

   Moth. Y'are welcome sir?

   Vind. The Next of *Italy* commends him to you,
Our mighty expectation, the Dukes sonne.

   Moth. I thinke my selfe much honord, that he pleases,
To ranck me in his thoughts.

  Vind. So may you Lady:
One that is like to be our suddaine Duke,
The Crowne gapes for him euery tide, and then
Commander ore vs all, do but thinke on him,
How blest were they now that could pleasure him
E'en with any thing almost.

   Moth. I, saue their honor?

  Vind. Tut, one would let a little of that go too
And nere be seene in't : nere be seene it, marke you,
Ide winck and let it go ————

   Moth. Marry but I would not.

  Vind. Marry but I would I hope, I know you would too,
If youd that bloud now which you gaue your daughter,
To her indeed tis, this wheele comes about,
That man that must be all this, perhaps ere morning
(For his white father do's but moulde away)
Has long desirde your daughter.   *Moth.* Desirde?

  Vind. Nay but heare me,
He desirs now that will command hereafter,
Therefore be wise, I speake as more a friend
To you then him; Madam, I know y'are poore,
And lack the day, there are too many poore Ladies already
Why should you vex the number? tis despisd,
Liue wealthy, rightly vnderstand the world,
And chide away that foolish--Country girle
Keepes company with your daughter, chastity,

   Moth. Oh fie, fie, the riches of the world cannot hire a mo-
ther to such a most vnnaturall taske.

   Vind. No, but a thousand Angells can,
Men haue no power, Angells must worke you too't,

The

The world defcends into fuch bafe-borne euills
That forty Angells can make fourefcore diuills,
There will be fooles ftill I perceiue,ftill foole.
Would I be poore deiected,fcornd of greatneffe,
Swept from the Pallace, and fee other daughters
Spring with the dewe ath Court,hauing mine owne
So much defir'd and lou'd---by the Dukes fonne,
No,I would raife my ftate vpon her breft
And call her eyes my Tennants, I would count
My yearely maintenance vpon her cheekes:
Take Coach vpon her lip,and all her partes
Should keepe men after men,and I would ride,
In pleafure vpon pleafure:
You tooke great paines for her,once when it was,
Let her requite it now,tho it be but fome
You brought her forth,fhe may well bring you home,
   Moth O heauens ! this ouer-comes me?
   Vind. Not I hope,already?
   Moth. It is too ftrong for me,men know that know vs,
We are fo weake their words can ouerthrow vs,
He toucht me neerely made my vertues bate
When his tongue ftruck vpon my poore eftate.
   Vind. I e'en quake to proceede,my fpirit turnes edge?
I feare me fhe's vnmotherd,yet ile venture,
,, That woman is all male,whome none can Enter?
What thinke you now Lady,fpeake are you wifer?
What fayd aduancement to you:thus it fayd!
The daughters fall lifts vp the mothers head:
Did it not Madame?but ile fweare it does
In many places,tut, this age feares no man,
,, Tis no fhame to be bad,becaufe tis common.
   Moth. I that's the comfort on't.
   Vind. The comfort on't!
I keepe the beft for laft,can thefe perfwade you
To forget heauen---and----   *Moth.* I thefe are they?
   Vind. Oh!
   Moth. That enchant our fexe,
Thefe are the means that gouerne our affections,--that woman
                                  Will

Will not be troubled with the mother long,
That fees the comfortable fhine of you,
I blufh to thinke what for your fakes Ile do!

 Vind. O fuffring heauen with thy inuifible finger,
Ene at this Inftant turne the pretious fide
Of both mine eye-bal's inward, not to fee my felfe,

 Mot. Looke you fir.   *Vin.* Holla.

 Mot. Let this thanke your paines.

 Vind. O you'r a kind Mad-man;

 Mot. Ile fee how I can moue,

 Vind. Your words will fting,

 Mot. If fhe be ftill chaft Ile nere call her mine,

 Vind Spoke truer then you ment it,

 Mot. Daughter *Caftiza.*   *Caft.* Madam,

 Vind. O fhees yonder.

Meete her: troupes of celeftiall Soldiers gard her heart,
Yon dam has deuills ynough to take her part,

 Caft. Madam what makes yon euill offic'd man,
In prefence of you;   *Mot.* Why?

 Caft. He lately brought
Immodeft writing fent from the Dukes fonne
To tempt me to difhonorable Act,

 Mot. Difhonorable Act?——good honorable foole,
That wouldft be honeft caufe thou wouldft be fo,
Producing no one reafon but thy will.
And t'as a good report, pretely commended,
But pray by whome; meane people; ignorant people,
The better fort Ime fure cannot abide it,
And by what rule fhouldft we fquare out our liues,
But by our betters actions? oh if thou knew'ft
What t'were to loofe it, thou would neuer keepe it:
But theres a cold curfe layd vpon all Maydes,
Whi'ft other clip the Sunne they clafp the fhades!
Virginity is paradice, lockt vp.
You cannot come by your felues without fee.
And twas decreed that man fhould keepe the key!
Deny aduancement, treafure, the Dukes fonne,

 Caft. I cry you mercy. Lady I miftooke you,

Pray

Pray did you fee my Mother ; which way went you ?
Pray God I haue not loſt her.

    Vind. Prittily put by.

    Moth. Are you as proud to me as coye to him ?
Doe you not know me now ?

    Caſt. Why are you ſhee ?
The worlds ſo changd, one ſhape into another,
It is a wiſe childe now that knowes her mother ?

    Vind. Moſt right ifaith.

    Mother. I owe your cheeke my hand,
For that preſumption now, but Ile forget it,
Come you ſhall leaue thoſe childiſh hauiours,
And vnderſtand your Time, Fortunes flow to you,
What will you be a Girle ?
If all feard drowning, that ſpye waues a ſhoare,
Gold would grow rich, and all the Marchants poore.

    Caſt. It is a pritty ſaying of a wicked one, but me thinkes now
It dos not ſhow ſo well out of your mouth,
Better in his.

    Vind. Faith bad inough in both,
Were I in earneſt as Ile ſeeme no leſſe ?
I wonder Lady your owne mothers words,
Cannot be taken, nor ſtand in full force.
'Tis honeſtie you vrge ; what's honeſtie ?
'Tis but heauens beggar ; and what woman is ſo fooliſh to
    keepe honeſty,
And be not able to keepe her-ſelfe ? No,
Times are growne wiſer and will keepe leſſe charge,
A Maide that h'as ſmall portion now entends,
To breake vp houſe, and liue vpon her friends
How bleſt are you, you haue happineſſe alone,
Others muſt fall to thouſands, you to one,
Sufficient in him-ſelfe to make your fore-head
Dazle the world with Iewels, and petitionary people
Start at your preſence.

    Mother. Oh if I were yong, I ſhould be rauiſht.

    Caſt. I to looſe your honour.

    Vind. Slid how can you looſe your honor?

D

To

To deale with my Lords Grace,
Heele adde more honour to it by his Title,
Your Mother will tell you how.

    Mother. That I will.

    Vind. O thinke vpon the pleasure of the Pallace,
Secured ease and state ; the stirring meates,   (their eaten,
Ready to moue out of the dishes, that e'en now quicken when
Banquets abroad by Torch-light, Musicks, sports,
Bare-headed vassailes, that had nere the fortune
To keepe on their owne Hats, but let hornes were em.
Nine Coaches waiting--hurry, hurry, hurry.

    Cast. I to the Diuill.

    Vind. I to the Diuill, toth' Duke by my faith.

    Moth. I to the Duke: daughter youde scorne to thinke ath'
Diuill and you were there once.

    Vin. True, for most there are as proud as he for his heart ifaith
Who'de sit at home in a neglected roome,
Dealing her short-liu'de beauty to the pictures,
That are as vse-lesse as old men, when those
Poorer in face and fortune then her-selfe,
Walke with a hundred Acres on their backs,
Faire Medowes cut into Greene fore-parts---oh
It was the greatest blessing euer happened to women;
When Farmers sonnes agreed, and met agen,
To wash their hands, and come vp Gentlemen;
The common-wealth has flourisht euer since,
Lands that were meat by the Rod, that labors spar'd,
Taylors ride downe, and measure em by the yeard;
Faire trees, those comely fore-tops of the Field,
Are cut to maintaine head-tires--much vntold,
All thriues but Chastity, she lyes a cold,
Nay sha'l I come neerer to you, marke but this:
Why are there so few honest women, but because 'tis the poorer
profession, that's accounted best, thats best followed, least in
trade, least in fashion, and thats not honesty beleeue it, and doe
but note the loue and deiected price of it:,

    Loose but a Pearle, we search and cannot brooke it.
    But that once gone, who is so mad to looke it.

                                    Mother

Mother. Troth he fayes true.

Caſt. Falſe, I defie you both :
I haue endur'd you with an eare of fire,
Your Tongues haue ſtruck hotte yrons on my face;
Mother, come from that poyſonous woman there.

Mother. Where ?

Caſt. Do you not ſee her, ſhee's too inward then :
Slaue periſh in thy office: you heauens pleaſe,
Hence-forth to make the Mother a diſeaſe,
Which firſt begins with me, yet I'ue out-gon you. *Exit.*

Vind. O Angels clap your wings vpon the skyes,
And giue this Virgin Chriſtall plaudities ?

Mot. Peeuiſh, coy, fooliſh, but returne this anſwer,
My Lord ſhall be moſt welcome, when his pleaſure
Conducts him this way, I will ſway mine owne,
Women with women can worke beſt alone. **Exit.**

Vind. Indeed Ile tell him ſo ;
O more vnciuill, more vnnaturall,
Then thoſe baſe-titled creatures that looke downe-ward,
Why do's not heauen tnrne black, or with a frowne
Vndoo the world—why do's not earth ſtart vp,
And ſtrike the ſinnes that tread vppon't—oh ;
Wert not for gold and women; there would be no damnation,
Hell would looke like a Lords Great Kitchin without fire in't;
But 'twas decreed before the world began,
That they ſhould be the hookes to catch, at man. **Exit.**

Enter Luſſurioſo , *with* Hippolito,
Vindicies *brother.*

Luſſ. I much applaud thy iudgement , thou art well read in a
fellow,
And 'tis the deepeſt Arte to ſtudie man;
I know this, which I neuer learnt in ſchooles,
The world's diuided into knaues and fooles.

Hip. Knaue in your face my Lord, behinde your back.

Luſſ. And I much thanke thee, that thou haſt preferd,
A fellow of diſcourſe—well mingled,
And whoſe braine Time hath ſeaſond.

Hip. True my Lord,

D 2

Wee

We shall finde season once I hope; --O villaine!
To make such an vnnaturall slaue of me ; --but---

Luss. Masse here he comes.

Hip. And now shall I haue free leaue to depart.

Luss. Your absence, leaue vs.

Hip. Are not my thoughts true ?

I must remooue ; but brother you may stay,
Heart, we are both made Bawdes a new-found way ?   *Exit.*

Luss. Now, we're an euen number ? a third mans dangerous,
Especially her brother, say, be free,
Haue I a pleasure toward.   *Vind.* Oh my Lord.

Luss. Rauish me in thine answer, art thou rare,
Hast thou beguilde her of saluation,
And rubd hell ore with hunny ; is she a woman ?

Vind. In all but in Desire.

Luss. Then shee's in nothing,---I bate in courage now.

Vind. The words I brought,
Might well haue made indifferent honest, naught,
A right good woman in these dayes is changde,
Into white money with lesse labour farre,
Many a Maide has turn'd to Mahomet,
With easier working ; I durst vndertake
Vpon the pawne and forfeit of my life.
With halfe those words to flat a Puritanes wife,
But she is closse and good ; --yet 'tis a doubt by this time ; oh
the mother, the mother ?

Luss. I neuer thought their sex had beene a wonder,
Vntill this minute ? what fruite from the Mother ?

Vind. Now must I blister my soule, be forsworne,
Or shame the woman that receiu'd mee first,
I will be true, thou liu'st not to proclaime,
Spoke to a dying man, shame ha's no shame.
My Lord.   *Luss.* Whose that ?

Vind. Heres none but I my Lord.

Luss. What would thy hast vtter ?

Vind. Comfort.   *Luss.* Welcome.

Vind. The Maide being dull, hauing no minde to trauell,
Into vnknowne lands, what did me I straight,

But

But set spurs to the Mother;golden spurs,
Will put her to a false gallop in a trice,

  *Luss.*Ist possible that in this.
The Mother should be dambd before the daughter?

  *Vin.*Oh, that's good manners my Lord , the Mother for her
age must goe formost you know.

  *Lu.*Thou'st spoke that true!but where comes in this comfort.

  *Vind.*In a fine place my Lord----the vnnaturall mother,
Did with her tong so hard be set her honor,
That the poore foole was struck to silent wonder,
Yet still the maid like an vnlighted Taper,
Was cold and chast,saue that her Mothers breath,
Did blowe fire on her checkes,the girle departed,
But the good antient Madam halfe mad,threwe me
These promissing words,which I tooke deepely note of;
My Lord shall be most wellcome,

  Luss Faith I thanke her,

  *Vin.*When his pleasure conducts him this way.

  *Luss.*That shall be soone ifath, *Vind.*I will sway mine owne,

  *Luss.*Shee do's the wiser I commend her fort,

  *Vind.*Women with women can worke best alone,

  *Luss.*By this light and so they can,giue 'em their due,men are
not comparable to 'em.

  Vind. No thats true , for you shall haue one woman knit
more in a hower then any man can Rauell agen in seauen and
twenty yeare.

  *Luss.*Now my desires are happy,Ile make 'em free-men now,
Thou art a pretious fellow,faith I loue thee,
Be wise and make it thy reuennew,beg,leg.
What office couldst thou be Ambitious for?

  Vind. Office my Lord marry if I might haue my wish I would
haue one that was neuer begd yet,

  *Luss.*Nay then thou canst haue none.

  Vind. Yes my Lord I could picke out another office yet, nay
and keepe a horse and drab vppont,

  *Luss.*Prethee good bluntnes tell me.

  Vind. Why I would desire but this my Lord , to haue all the
fees behind the *Arras* ; and all the farthingales that fal plumpe

                about

about twelue a clock at night vpon the Rushes.

Luss. Thou'rt a mad apprehensiue knaue, dost thinke to make
any great purchase of that.

Vind. Oh tis an vnknowne thing my Lord, I wonder ta's been
mist so long?

Luss. Well, this night ile visit her, and tis till then
A yeare in my desires--farwell, attend,
Trust me with thy preferment.   **Exit.**

Vind. My lou'd Lord;
Oh shall I kill him ath wrong-side now, no!
Sword thou wast neuer a back-biter yet,
Ile peirce him to his face, he shall die, looking vpon me,
Thy veines are sweld with lust, this shall vnfill e'm,
Great men were Gods, if beggers could not kil e'm,
Forgiue me heauen, to call my mother wicked,
Oh lessen not my daies vpon the earth
I cannot honor her, by this I feare me
Her tongue has turnd my sister into vse.
I was a villaine not to be forsworne:
To this our lecherous hope, the Dukes sonne,
For Lawiers, Merchants, some diuines and all,
Count beneficiall periury a sin small,
It shall go hard yet, but ile guard her honor
And keepe the portes sure?   *Enter* **Hippol.**

Hip. Brother how goes the world? I would know newes of you
But I haue newes to tell you.

Vind. What in the name of knauery?

Hipo. Knauery fayth,
This vicious old Duke's worthily abusde
The pen of his bastard writes him Cuckold!

Vind. His bastard?

Hip. Pray beleeue it, he and the Duchesse,
By night meete in their linnen, they haue beene seene
By staire-foote pandars!

Vind. Oh sin foule and deepe,
Great faults are winckt at when the **Duke's a sleepe**,
See see here comes the *Spurio.*

Hip. **Monstrous Luxur?**

                                                    Vind.

Vind. Vnbrac'd:two of his valiant bawdes with him,
O There's a wicked whisper;hell is in his eare.
Stay let's obserue his passage ⸺⸺
  Spu. Oh but are you sure on't.
  Ser. My Lord most sure on't , for twas spoke by one,
That is most inward with the Dukes sonnes lust:
That he intends within this houre to steale,
Vnto *Hippolitoes* sister,whose chast life
The mother has corrupted for his vse.
Sp. Sweete world,sweeter occasió, sayth then brother
Ile disinherit you in as short time,
As I was when I was begot in hast:
Ile dam you at your pleasure : pretious deed
After your lust,oh twill be fine to bleede,
Come let our passing out be soft & wary.   *Exeunt.*
  Vi. Marke,there,there,that step,now to the Duches,
This their second meeting,writes the Duke Cuckold
With new additions his hornes newly reuiu'd:
Night!thou that lookst like funerall Heraulds fees
Torne downe betimes ith morning, thou hangst fittly
To Grace those sins that haue no grace at all,
Now tis full sea a bed ouer the world,
Theres iugling of all sides, some that were Maides
E'en at Sun set are now perhaps ith Toale-booke,
This woman in immodest thin apparell:
Lets in her friend by water,here a Dame
Cunning,nayles lether-hindges to a dore,
To auoide proclamation,
Now Cuckolds are a quoyning,apace,apace,apace,apace
And carefull sisters spinne that thread ith night,
That does maintaine them and their bawdes ith daie!
  Hip. You flow well brother?
  Vind. Puh I'me shallow yet,
Too sparing and too modest,shall I tell thee,
If euery trick were told that's dealt by night
There are few here that would not blush out right.
  Hip. I am of that beleefe too.
  Vind. Whose this comes,

The

Vind. The Dukes fonne vp fo late,--brother fall back,
And you fhall learne, fome mifcheife,---my good Lord.

  Luff. Pirto, why the man I wifht for , come,
I do embrace this feafon for the fitteft
To taft of that yong Lady?   *Vind.* Heart, and hell.

  Hip. Dambd villaine.

  Vind. ₁ ha no way now to croffe it, but to kill him.

  Lufs. Come only thou and I.   *Vin.* My Lord my Lord.

  Lufs. Why doft thou ftart vs?

  Vind. Ide almoft forgot---the baftard!   *Luf.* What of him?

  Vind. This night, this houre ---this minute, now.

  Lufs. What? what?   *Vin.* Shadowes the Ducheffe----

  Lufs. Horrible word.

  Vind. And like ftrong poyfon cates,
Into the Duke your fathers fore-head.   *Lufs.* Oh.

  Vind. He makes horne royall.   *Luf:.* Moft ignoble flaue?

  Vind. This is the fruite of two beds.   *Lufs.* I am mad.

  Vind. That paffage he trod warily: *Lufs.* He did!

  Vind. And hufht his villaines euery ftep he tooke.

  Lufs. His villaines? ile confound them.

  Vind. Take e'm finely, finely, now.

  Luff. The Ducheffe Chamber-doore fhall not controule mee.

  Hip. Good, happy, fwift, there's gunpowder ith Court, (*Exeunt*
Wilde fire at mid-night, in this heedleffe fury
He may fhow violence to croffe himfelfe,
Ile follow the Euent.   *Exit.*

  Luff. Where is that villaine?   *Enter againe.*

  Vind. Softly my Lord and you may take e'm twifted.

  Luff. I care not how!

  Vind. Oh twill be glorious,
To kill e'm doubled, when their heapt, be foft my Lord.

  Luff Away my pleene is not fo lazy, thus and thus,
Ile fhake their eye-lids ope, and with my fword
Shut e'm agen for euer;---villaine, ftrumpet ————

  Duk. You vpper Guard defend vs.   *Duch.* Treafon, treafon.

  Duk. Oh take mee not in fleepe, I haue great fins, I muft haue
Nay months deere fonne, with penitential heaues,   (daies,
To lift 'em out, and not to die vncleere,

                                                O

O thou wilt kill me both in heauen and here.

Luſſ. I am amazde to death.

Duke Nay villaine traytor,
Worſe then the fowleſt Epithite, now Ile gripe thee
Ee'n with the Nerues of wrath, and throw thy head
Amongſt the Lawyers gard.

Enter Nobles and ſonnes.

1. *Noble.* How comes the quiet of your Grace diſturbd?

Duke. This boye that ſhould be my ſelfe after mee,
Would be my ſelfe before me, and in heate
Of that ambition bloudily ruſht in
Intending to depoſe me in my bed?

2. *Noble.* Duty and naturall-loyalty for-fend.

Dut. He cald his Father villaine; and me ſtrumpet,
A word that I abhorre to file my lips with.

Ambi. That was not ſo well done Brother?

Luſſ. I am abuſde--I know ther's no excuſe can do me good.

Vind. Tis now good policie to be from ſight,
His vicious purpoſe to our ſiſters honour,
Is croſt beyond our thought.

Hip. You little dreamt his Father ſlept heere.

Vind. Oh 'twas farre beyond me.
But ſince it fell ſo; --without fright-full word,
Would he had kild him, twould haue eaſde our ſwords.

Duk. Be comforted our Ducheſſe, he ſhall dye. *diſſemble a*

Luſſ. Where's this ſlaue-pander now? out of mine eye, *flight.*
Guiltie of this abuſe.

Enter Spurio with his villaines.

Spu. Y'are villaines, Fablers,
You haue knaues chins, and harlots tongues, you lie,
And I wlll dam you with one meale a day.

1. *Ser.* O good my Lord!

Spu. Sbloud you ſhall neuer ſup.

2. *Ser.* O I beſeech you ſir.

Spu. To let my ſword--- Catch cold ſo long and miſſe him.

1. *Ser.* Troth my Lord--Twas his intent ro meete there.

Spu. Heart hee s yonder?

Ha? what newes here? is the day out ath-ſocket,

E   That

That it is Noone at Mid-night; the Court vp,
How comes the Guard so sawcie with his elbowes ?

Luss. The Bastard here ?
Nay then the truth of my intent shall out,
My Lord and Father heare me.   *Duke.* Beare him hence.

Luss. I can with loyaltie excuse.

Duke. Excuse ? to prison with the Villaine,
Death shall not long lag after him.

Spu. Good ifaith, then 'tis not much amisse,

Luss. Brothers, my best release lies on your tongues,
I pray perswade for mee.

Ambi. It is our duties : make your selfe sure of vs.

Sup. Weele sweate in pleading.

Luss. And I may liue to thanke you.   *Exeunt.*

Ambi. No, thy death shall thanke me better.

Spu. Hee's gon : Ile after him,
And know his trespasse, seeme to beare a part
In all his ills, but with a *Puritane* heart.   *Exit.*

Amb. Now brother, let our hate and loue be wouen
So subtilly together, that in speaking one word for his life,
We may make three for his death.
The craftiest pleader gets most gold for breath.

Sup. Set on, Ile not be farre behinde you brother.

Duke. Ist possible a sonne should bee disobedient as farre as
the sword : it is the highest he can goe no farther.

Ambi. My gratious Lord, take pitty,---   *Duke.* Pitty boyes ?

Amb. Nay weed be loth to mooue your Grace too much,
Wee know the trespasse is vnpardonable,
Black, wicked, and vnnaturall,

Sup In a Sonne, oh Monstrous.

Ambi. Yet my Lord,
A Dukes soft hand stroakes the rough head of law,
And makes it lye smooth.   *Duk* But my hand shall nere doot.

Amb. That as you please my Lord.

Super. Wee must needs confesse,
Some father would haue enterd into hate,
So deadly pointed, that before his eyes,
Hee would ha seene the execution sound,

                                                Withou

Without corrupted fauour?

Amb. But my Lord,
Your Grace may liue the wonder of all times,
In pardning that offence which neuer yet
Had face to beg a pardon.   *Duke.* Hunny, how's this?

   Amb. Forgiue him good my Lord, hee s your owne sonne,
And I must needs say 'twas the vildlier done.

   Superv. Hee's the next heire--yet this true reason gathers,
None can possesse that dispossesse their fathers:
Be mercifull; ———

   Duke. Here's no Step-mothers-wit,
Ile trie em both vpon their loue and hate.

   Amb. Be mercifull--altho--   *Duke.* You haue preuaild,
My wrath like flaming waxe hath spent it selfe,   (releasd.
I know 'twas but some peeuish Moone in him: goe, let him bee

   Superv. Stoote how now Brother?

   Amb. Your Grace doth please to speake beside your spleene,
I would it were so happy?   *Duke.* Why goe, release him.

   Superv. O my good Lord, I know the fault's too weighty,
And full of generall loathing; too inhumaine,
Rather by all mens voyces worthy death.

   Duke. Tis true too; here then, receiue this signet, doome shall
Direct it to the Iudges, he shall dye   (passe,
Ere many dayes, make hast.

   Amb. All speed that may be,
We could haue wisht his burthen not so sore,
We knew your Grace did but delay before.   *Exeunt.*

   Duke. Here's Enuie with a poore thin couer or't,
Like Scarlet hid in lawne, easily spide through,
This their ambition by the Mothers side,
Is dangerous, and for safetie must be purgd,
I will preuent their enuies, sure it was
But some mistaken furie in our sonne,
Which these aspiring boyes would climbe vpon:
He shall bee releasde suddainly.   *Enter Nobles.*

   1. *Nob.* Good morning to your Grace.

   Duke. Welcome my Lords.   (euer,
   2. *Nob.* Our knees shall take away the office of our feete for

    Vnlesse

Vnlesse your Grace bestow a fathers eye,
Vpon the Clouded fortunes of your sonne,
And in compassionate vertue grant him that,
Which makes e'en meane men happy; liberty
   Duk. How seriously their loues and honors woo
For that, which I am about to pray them doo
Which, rise my Lords, your knees signe his release,
We freely pardon him.
   1.Nob. We owe your Grace much thankes, and he much duety.
   Duk. It well becomes that Iudge to nod at crimes,   (*Exeunt.*
That dos commit greater himselfe and liues:
I may forgiue a disobedient error,
That expect pardon for adultery
And in my old daies am a youth in lust:
Many a beauty haue I turnd to poyson
In the deniall, couetous of all,
Age hot, is like a Monster to be seene:
My haires are white, and yet my sinnes are Greene.

ACT. 3.

Enter Ambitioso, *and* Supernacuo?

   Sup. Brother, let my opinion sway you once,
I speake it for the best, to haue him die:
Surest and soonest, if the signet come,
Vnto the iudges hands, why then his doome,
Will be deferd till sittings and Court-daies:
Iuries and further,--Fayths are bought and sold,
Oths in these daies are but the skin of gold.
   Amb. In troth tis true too!
   Super. Then lets set by the Iudges
And fall to the Officers, tis but mistaking
The Duke our fathers meaning, and where he nam'd,
Ere many daies, tis but forgetting that
And, haue him die i'th morning.
   Amb. Excellent,
Then am I heire--Duke in a minute.
   Super. Nay,
And he were once pufft out, here is a pinne.

                                  Should

Should quickly prick your bladder.

Amb. Blaſt occaſion,
He being packt, weele haue ſome trick and wile,
To winde our yonger brother out of priſon,
That lies in for the Rape, the Ladies dead,
And peoples thoughts will ſoone be buried.

Super. We may with ſafty do't, and liue and feede,
The Ducheſſe-ſonnes are too proud to bleed,

Am. We are yfaith to ſay true.—come let's not linger
Ile to the Cfficers, go you before,
And ſet an edge vpon the Executioner.

Sup. Let me alone to grind him.   *Exit.*

Amb. Meete; farewell,
I am next now, I riſe iuſt in that place,
Where thou'lt cut of, vpon thy Neck kind brother,
The falling of one head, lifts vp another.   *Exit.*

    Enter with the Nobles, Luſſurioſo *from pryſon.*

Luſſ. My Lords? I am ſo much indebted to your loues,
For this, O this deliuery.

   1. *Nob.* But our dueties, my Lord, vnto the hopes that growe

Luſſ. If ere I liue to be my ſelfe ile thanke you,   (in you,
O liberty thou ſweete and heauenly Dame;
But hell for pryſon is too milde a name.   *Exeunt.*

    Enter Ambitioſo, *and* Superuacuo? *with Officers.*

Am. Officers? heres the Dukes ſignet, your firme warrant,
Brings the command of preſent death a long with it
Vnto our brother, the Dukes ſonne; we are ſory,
That we are ſo vnnaturally employde
In ſuch an vnkinde Office, fitter farre
For enemies then brothers.

Super. But you know,
The Dukes command muſt be obayde.

   1. *Offi.* It muſt and ſhal my Lord—this morning then,
So ſuddainely?

   Am. I alaſſe poore—good—ſoule,
Hee muſt breake faſt betimes, the executioner
Stands ready to put forth his cowardly valour.

   2. *Offi.* Already?

Sup. Alreardy ifath, O fir, deftruction hies,
And that is leaft Impudent, fooneft dyes,

    1. *Off.* Troth you fay true my Lord we take **our leaues,**
Our Office fhall be found, weele not delay,
The third part of a minute.

    Amb. Therein you fhowe.
Your felues good men, and vpright officers,
Pray let him die as priuat as he may,
Doe him that fauour, for the gaping people.
Will but trouble him at his prayers,
And make him curfe, and fweare, and fo die black.
Will you be fo far Kind?

    1. *Off.* It fhall be done my Lord.
    Amb. Why we do thanke you, if we liue to be,
You fhall haue a better office,

    2. *Off.* Your good Lord-fhippe.
    Sup. Commend vs to the fcaffold in our teares.

    1. *Off* Weele weepe and doe your commendations,   *Exeunt.*
    Amb. Fine fooles in office!   *Sup.* Things fall out fo fit.
    Amb. So happily, come brother ere next clock,
His head will be made ferue a bigger block.   **Exeunt.**

          Enter in prifon Iunior *Brother,*
Iuni. Keeper.   *Keep.* My Lord.
    Iuni. No newes lately from our brothers?
Are they vnmindfull of vs?   (from 'em,
    Keep. My Lord a meffenger came newly in and brought this
    Iuni. Nothing but paper comforts?
I look'd for my deliuery before this,
Had they beene worth their oths---prethee be from **vs.**
Now what fay you forfooth, fpeake out I pray,
          Letter. Brother be of good cheere,
Slud it begins like a whore with good cheere,
       Thou fhalt not be long a prifoner.
Not fiue and thirty yeare like a banqrout, I thinke fo,
    We haue thought vpon a deuice to get thee out by a tricke!
By a tricke, pox a your tricke and it be fo long a playing.
     And fo reft comforted, be merry and expect it fuddaynely!
Be merry, hang merry, draw and quarter merry, Ile be mad!

                                            ift

Ift not ftrange that a man fhould lie in a whole month for a wo-
man, well,wee fhall fee how fuddaine our brothers:will bee in
their promife , I muft expect ftill a trick ! I fhall not bee long a
prifoner,how now,what newes?

 Keeper. Bad newes my Lord I am difcharg'd of you.

 Iunio. Slaue calft thou that bad newes,I thanke you brothers.

 Keep. My Lord twill proue fo,here come the Officers,
Into whofe hands I muft commit you.

 Iunio. Ha,Officers,what,why?

 1 *Offi.* You muft pardon vs my Lord,
Our Office muft be found,here is our warrant
The fignet from the Duke,you muft ftraight fuffer.

 Iunior. Suffer? ile fuffer you to be gon,ile fuffer you,
To come no more,what would you haue me fuffer?

 2. *Offi.* My Lord thofe words were better chang'd to praiers,
The times but breife with you,prepare to die.

 Iunior. Sure tis not fo.   3.*Offi.* It is too true my Lord.

 Iunior. I tell you tis not,for the Duke my father,
Deferd me till next fitting, and I looke
E'en euery minute threefcore times an houre,
For a releafe,a trick wrought by my brothers.

 1.*Offi.* A trick my Lord?if you expect fuch comfort,
Your hopes as fruitleffe as a barren woman:
Your brothers were the vnhappy meffengers,
That brought this powerfull token for your death.

 Iunior. My brothers,no,no.

 2.*Offi.* Tis moft true my Lord.

 Iunior. My brothers to bring a warrant for my death
How ftrange this fhowes?

 3.*Offi.* There's no delaying time.

 Iunior. Defire e'm hether,call e'm vp,my brothers?
They fhall deny it to your faces.

 1.*Offi.* My Lord,
They're far ynough by this,at leaft at Court,
And this moft ftrickt command they left behinde e'm,
When griefe fwum in their eyes,they fhow'd like brothers,
Brim-full of heauy forrow:but the Duke
Muft haue his pleafure. *Iunio.* His pleafure?

           1.*Offi.*

1.*Off.* Thefe were their laft words which my memory beares,
Commend vs to the Scaffold in our teares.

Iunior. Pox drye their teares,what fhould I do with teares?
I hate em worfe then any Cittizens fonne
Can hate falt water; here came a letter now,
New-bleeding from their Pens,fcarce ftinted yet,
Would Ide beene torne in pecces when I tore it,
Looke you officious whorefons words of comfort,
Not long a Prifoner.

1.*Off.* It fayes true in that fir,for you muft fuffer prefently.

Iunior. A villanous Duns,vpon the letter knauifh expofition,
Looke you then here fir: *Weele get thee ont by a trick fayes bee.*

2.*Off.* That may hold too fir, for you know a Trick is com-
monly foure Cardes,which was meant by vs foure officers.

Iunior. Worfe and worfe dealing.

1.*Off.* The houre beckens vs,
The headf-man waites, lift vp your eyes to heauen.

Iunior. I thanke you faith; good pritty-holfome counfell,
I fhould looke vp to heauen as you fedd,
Whilft he behinde me cozens me of my head,
I thats the Trick.　　　3.*Off.* You delay too long my Lord.

Iunior. Stay good Authorities Baftards,fince I muft
Through Brothers periurie dye, O let me venome
Their foules with curfes.　　1.*Off.*Come tis no time to curfe.

Iunior. Muft I bleed then, without refpect of figne? well——
My fault was fweet fport,which the world approoues,
I dye for that which euery woman loues.　　　*Exeunt.*

　　　　　Enter Vindici *with* Hippolito *his brother.*

Vind. O fweete,delectable,rare,happy,rauifhing,

Hip. Why what's the matter brother?

Vin. O tis able,to make a man fpring vp,& knock his for-head
Againft yon filuar feeling.

Hip. Pre-thee tell mee,
Why may not I pertake with you?you vowde once
To giue me fhare to euery tragick thought.

Vind. Byth' Maffe I thinke I did too,
Then Ile diuide it to thee,---the old Duke
Thinking my outward fhape,and inward heart

Are cut out of one peice; (for he that prates his secrets,
His heart stands ath out side)hires me by price:
To greete him with a Lady,
In some fit place vaylde from the eyes ath Court,
Some darkned blushlesse Angle,that is guilty
Of his fore-fathers lusts,and great-folkes riots,
To which(I easily to maintaine my shape)
Consented, and did wish his impudent grace
To meete her here in this vn-sunned-lodge,
Where-in tis night at noone, and here the rather,
Because vnto the torturing of his soule,
The Bastard and the Duchesse haue appoynted
Their meeting too in this luxurious circle,
Which most afflicting sight will kill his eyes
Before we kill the rest of him.

   Hip. Twill yfaith,most dreadfully digested,
I see not how you could haue mist me brother.
    Vind. True,but the violence of my ioy forgot it.
    Hip. I,but where's that Lady now?
    Vind. Oh at that word,
I'me lost againe, you cannot finde me yet
I'me in a throng of happy Apprehensions
Hee's suted for a Lady,I haue tooke care
For a delitious lip,a sparkling eye,
You shall be witnesse brother;
Be ready stand with your hat off.   *Exit.*

   Hip. Troth I wonder what Lady it should be?
Yet tis no wonder,now I thinke againe,
To haue a Lady stoope to a Duke,that stoopes vnto his men,
Tis common to be common,through the world:
And there's more priuate common shadowing vices,
Then those who are knowne both by their names and prices
Tis part of my alleagance to stand bare,
To the Dukes Concubine,—and here she comes.
     Enter Vindice,*with the skull of his loue drest vp in Tires.*
    Vind. Madame his grace will not be absent long.
Secret ? nere doubt vs Madame ? twill be worth
Three veluet gownes to your Ladyship—knowne?

Few Ladies respect that? disgrace, a poore thin shell,
Tis the best grace you haue to do it well,
Ile saue your hand that labour, ile vnmaske you?

   Hip. Why brother, brother.

   Vind. Art thou beguild now? tut, a Lady can,
At such all hid, beguile a wiser man,
Haue I not fitted the old surfeiter
With a quaint peice of beauty, age and bare bone
Are ere allied in action; here's an eye,
Able to tempt a greatman--to serue God,
A prety hanging lip, that has forgot now to dissemble
Me thinkes this mouth should make a swearer tremble.
A drunckard claspe his teeth, and not vndo e'm,
To suffer wet damnation to run through e'm.
Heres a cheeke keepes her colour let the winde go whistle,
Spout Raine, we feare thee not, be hot or cold
Alls one with vs; and is not he absur'd,
Whose fortunes are vpon their faces set,
That feare no other God but winde and wet.

   Hip. Brother y'aue spoke that right,
Is this the forme that liuing shone so bright?

   Vind. The very same,
And now me thinkes I cold e'en chide my selfe,
For doating on her beauty, tho her death
Shall be reuengd after no common action;
Do's the Silke-worme expend her yellow labours
For thee? for thee dos she vndoe herselfe?
Are Lord-ships sold to maintaine Lady-ships
For the poore benefit of a bewitching minute?
Why dos yon fellow falsify' hie-waies
And put his life betweene the Iudges lippes,
To refine such a thing, keepes horse and men
To beate their valours for her?
Surely wee're all mad people, and they
Whome we thinke are, are not, we mistake those,
Tis we are mad in scence, they but in clothes.

   Hip. Faith and in clothes too we, giue vs our due.

   Vind. Dos euery proud and selfe-affecting Dame

                             Camphire

Camphire her face for this?an dgrieue her Maker
In sinfull baths of milke,--when many an infant starues,
For her superfluous out-side, all for this?
Who now bids twenty pound a night,prepares
Musick,perfumes,and sweete-meates,all are husht,
Thou maist lie chast now ! it were fine me thinkes:
To haue thee seene at Reuells, forgetfull feasts,
And vncleane Brothells ; sure twould fright the sinner
And make him a good coward,put a Reueller,
Out off his Antick amble
And cloye an Epicure with empty dishes?
Here might a scornefull and ambitious woman,
Looke through and through her selfe, ---see Ladies , with false
You deceiue men, but cannot deceiue wormes.   (formes,
Now to my tragick businesse,looke you brother,
I haue not fashiond this onely—for show
And vselesse property,no,it shall beare a part
E'en in it owne Reuenge.This very skull,
Whose Mistris the Duke poysoned,with this drug
The mortall curse of the earth ; shall be reuengd
In the like straine, and kisse his lippes to death,
As much as the dumbe thing can, he shall feele:
What fayles in poyson, weele supply in steele.
  Hip. Brother I do applaud thy constant vengeance,
The quaintnesse of thy malice aboue thought.
  Vind. So tis layde on : now come and welcome Duke,
I haue her for thee,I protest it brother:
Me thinkes she makes almost as faire a fine
As some old gentlewoman in a Periwig?
Hide thy face now for shame , thou hadst neede haue a Maske
Tis vaine when beauty flowes,but when it fleetes   (now
This would become graues better then the streetes.
  Hip. You haue my voice in that; harke,the Duke's come.
  Vind. Peace,let's obserue what company he brings,
And how he dos absent e'm , for you knowe
Heele wish all priuate ,--brother fall you back a little,
With the bony Lady.   Hip. That I will.
  Vind. So,so,--now 9.years vengeance crowde into a minute!

Duk. You shall haue leaue to leaue vs,with this charge,
Vpon your liues,if we be mist by'th Duchesse
Or any of the Nobles,to giue out,
We're priuately rid forth.   *Vind.* Oh happinesse!

   Duk. With some few honorable gentlemen you may say,
You may name those that are away from Court.

   Gentle. Your will and pleasure shall be done my Lord.

   Vind. Priuately rid forth,
He striues to make sure worke on't—your good grace?

   Duk. *Piato*, well done hast brought her,what Lady ist?

   Vind. Faith my Lord a Country Lady,a little bashfull at first
as most of them are, but after the first kisse my Lord the worst is
past with them,your grace knowes now what you haue to doo;
sha's some-what a graue looke with her—but ————————

   Duk. I loue that best,conduct her.

   Vind. Haue at all.

   Duk. In grauest lookes the Greatest faultes seeme lesse
Giue me that sin thats rob'd in Holines.

   Vind. Back with the Torch ; brother raise the perfumes.

   Duk. How sweete can a Duke breath ? age has no fault,
Pleasure should meete in a perfumed mist,
Lady sweetely encountred,I came from Court I must bee bould
with you,oh,what's this,oh!

   Vind. royall villaine,white diuill;   *Duke.* Oh.

   Vind. Brother—place the Torch here,that his affrighted eye-
May start into those hollowes,Duke;dost knowe   (balls
Yon dreadfull vizard,view it well,tis the skull
Of *Gloriana*,whom thou poysonedst last.

   Duk. Oh , tas poysoned me.

   Vind. Didst not know that till now?

   Duk. What are you two?

   Vind. Villaines all three:—the very ragged bone,
Has beene sufficiently reuengd.

   Duk. Oh *Hippolito*?call treason.

   Hip. Yes my good Lord, treason,treason,treason. *stamping*
   Duk. Then I'me betrayde.   *on him.*

   Vind. Alasse poore Lecher in the hands of knaues,
A slauish Duke is baser then his slaues.

                          Duke.

Duke. My teeth are eaten out.　　*Vind.* Hadſt any left.

Hip. I thinke but few.

Vin. Then thoſe that did eate are eaten.　*Duk.* O my tongue.

Vind. Your tongue? twill teach you to kiſſe cloſer,

Not like a Flobbering *Dutchman*, you haue eyes ſtill :

Looke monſter, what a Lady haſt thou made me,

My once bethrothed wife.

　Duk. Is it thou villaine, nay then----

　Vind. T'is I, 'tis *Vindici*, tis I .

　Hip. And let this comfort thee : our Lord and Father

Fell ſick vpon the infection of thy frownes,

And dyed in ſadneſſe ; be that thy hope of life.　*Duke.* Oh?

　Vind. He had his toung, yet greefe made him die ſpeechleſſe.

Puh, tis but early yet, now ile begin

To ſtick thy ſoule with Vlcers, I will make

Thy ſpirit grieuous ſore, it ſhall not reſt,

But like ſome peſtilent man toſſe in thy breſt- (marke me duke)

Thou'rt a renowned, high, and mighty Cuckold.　*Duke.* Oh!

　Vind. Thy Baſtard, thy baſtard rides a hunting in thy browe.

　Duke. Millions of deaths.

　Vind. Nay to afflict thee more,

Here in this lodge they meete for damned clips,

Thoſe eyes ſhall ſee the inceſt of their lips.

　Duke. Is there a hell beſides this, villaines ? *Vind.* Villaine ?

Nay heauen is iuſt, ſcornes are the hires of ſcornes,

I nere knew yet Adulterer with-out hornes.

　Hip. Once ere they dye 'tis quitted.

　Vind. Harke the muſicke,

Their banquet is preparde, they're comming ————

　Duke. Oh, kill me not with that ſight.

　Vin. Thou ſhalt not looſe that ſight for all thy Duke-doome.

　Duke. Traytors, murderers ?

　Vin. What ? is not thy tongue eaten out yet ?

Then weele inuent a ſilence ? brother ſtifle the Torch,

　Duke. Treaſon, murther ?

　Vind. Nay faith, weele haue you huſht now with thy dagger

Naile downe his tongue, and mine ſhall keepe poſſeſſion

About his heart, if hee but gaſpe hee dyes,

Wee dread not death to quittance iniuries;---Brother,
If he but winck, not brooking the foule obiect,
Let our two other hands teare vp his lids,
And make his eyes like Comets shine through bloud,
When the bad bleedes, then is the Tragedie good,
   Hip. Whist, brother, musick's at our eare, they come.
      Enter the Bastard meeting the Dutchesse.
   Spu. Had not that kisse a taste of sinne 'twere sweete.
   Dutch. Why there's no pleasure sweet but it is sinfull.
   Spu. True, such a bitter sweetnesse fate hath giuen,
Best side to vs, is the worst side to heauen.
   Dutch. Push, come : 'tis the old Duke thy doubtfull Father,
The thought of him rubs heauen in thy way,
But I protest by yonder waxen fire,
Forget him, or ile poyson him.
   Spu. Madam, you vrge a thought which nere had life,
So deadly doe I loath him for my birth,
That if hee tooke mee haspt within his bed,
I would adde murther to adultery,
And with my sword giue vp his yeares to death.
   Dutch. Why now thou'rt sociable, lets in and feast,
Lowdst Musick sound : pleasure is Banquests guest.   *Exeunt.*
   Duk. I cannot brooke----*Vind.* The Brooke is turnd to bloud.
   Hip. Thanks to lowd Musick.   *Vind.* Twas our friend indeed,
'Tis state in Musicke for a Duke to bleed :
The Duke-dome wants a head, tho yet vnknowne,
As fast as they peepe vp, lets cut 'em downe.   *Exeunt.*
    Enter the Dutchesse two sonnes, Ambitioso & Supervacuo.
   Amb. Was not his execution rarely plotted?
We are the Dukes sonnes now.
   Super. I you may thanke my policie for that.
   Amb. Your policie, for what ?
   Super. Why wast not my inuention brother,
To slip the Iudges, and in lesser compasse,
Did not I draw the modell of his death,
Aduizing you to suddaine officers,
And een extemporall execution.
   Amb. Heart, twas a thing I thought on too.

                                      Super.

Sup. You thought ont too, ffoote flander not your thoughts
With glorious vntruth, I know twas from you.

Amb. Sir I fay, twas in my head.

Spu. I, like your braines then,
Nere to come out as long as you liu'd.

Amb. You'd haue the honor on't forfooth, that your wit
Lead him to the fcaffold,

Super. Since it is my due,
Ile publifht, but Ile ha't in fpite of you.

Amb. Me thinkes y'are much too bould, you fhould a little
Remember vs brother, next to be honeft Duke.

Sup. I, it fhall be as eafie for you to be Duke,
As to be honeft, and that's neuer ifaith.

Amb. Well, cold he is by this time, and becaufe
Wee're both ambitious, be it our amity,
And let the glory be fharde equally. *Sup.* I am content to that.

Amb. This night our yonger brother fhall out of prifon,
I haue a trick.   *Sup.* A trick, pre-thee what ift?

Amb. Weele get him out by a wile. *Sup.* Pre-thee what wile?

Amb. No fir, you fhall not know it, till't be done,
For then you'd fweare twere yours.

Super. How now, whats he?   *Amb.* One of the officers.

Super. Defired newes.   *Amb.* How now my friend?

Off. My Lords, vnder your pardon, I am allotted
To that defertleffe office, to prefent you
With the yet bleeding head.   *Sup.* Ha, ha, excellent.

Amb. All's fure our owne: Brother, canft weepe thinkft thou?
Twould grace our Flattery much; thinke of fome Dame,
Twill teach thee to diffemble.

Sup. I haue thought,--Now for your felfe.

Amb. Our forrowes are fo fluent,
Our eyes ore-flow our toungs, words fpoake in teares,
Are like the murmures of the waters, the found
Is lowdly heard, but cannot be diftinguifht.

Sup. How dyed he pray?   *Off.* O full of rage and fpleene.

Super. He dyed moft valiantly then, we're glad to heare it.

Off. We could not woe him once to pray.   (due.

Amb. He fhowd himfelfe a Gentleman in that: giue him his
                                                Off. But

Off. But in the steed of prayer, he drew forth oaths.

Super. Then did hee pray deere heart,
Although you vnderstood him not.

Offi. My Lords,
E'en at his last, with pardon bee it spoake,
Hee curst you both.

Sup. Hee curst vs? lasse good soule.

Amb It was not in our powers, but the Dukes pleasure,
Finely dissembled a both-sides, sweete fate,
O happy opportunitie.   *Enter* Lussurioso.

Luss. Now my Lords.   *Both.* Oh! ————

Luss. Why doe you shunne mee Brothers?
You may come neerer now;
The sauor of the prison has for-sooke mee,
I thanke such kinde Lords as your selues, Ime free.

Amb Aliue!   *Super.* In health!

Amb. Releasd?
We were both ee'n amazd with ioy to see it,

Luss. I am much to thanke you.

Sup. Faith we spar'd no toung, vnto my Lord the Duke.

Amb. I know your deliuery brother
Had not beene halfe so sudden but for vs.

Sup. O how we pleaded.   *Luss.* Most deseruing brothers,
In my best studies I will thinke of it?   *Exit* Luss.

Amb. O death and vengeance.   *Sup.* Hell and torments.

Amb. Slaue camst thou to delude vs.   *Off.* Delude you my

Super. I villaine, where's this head now?   (Lords?

Off. Why heere my Lord,
Iust after his deliuery, you both came
With warrant from the Duke to be-head your brother.

Amb. I, our brother, the Dukes sonne.

Off. The Dukes sonne my Lord, had his release before you

Amb. Whose head's that then?   (came.

Off. His whom you left command for, your owne brothers?

Amb. Our brothers? oh furies ————

Sup. Plagues.   *Amb.* Confusions.

Sup. Darkenesse.   *Amb.* Diuils.

Sup. Fell it out so accursedly?   *Amb.* So damnedly.

                                                                    Super.

Sup. Villaine Ile braine thee with it, *Off.* O my good Lord!

Sup. The Diuill ouer-take thee?   *Amb.* O fatall.

Sup. O prodigious to our blouds.   *Amb.* Did we diffemble?

Sup. Did we make our teares woemen for thee?

Amb. Laugh and reioyce for thee.

Sup. Bring warrant for thy death.   *Amb.* Mock off thy head

Super. You had a trick, you had a wile forfooth.

Amb. A murren meete 'em, there's none of; thefe wiles that euer come to good : I fee now, there is nothing fure in mortali-tie, but mortalitie, well, no more words fhalt be reuengd ifaith. Come, throw off clouds now brother, thinke of vengeance, And deeper fetled hate, firrah fit faft, Weele pull downe all, but thou fhalt downe at laft.   *Exeunt.*

ACT.4. SCEN.1.

Enter Luffurioſo *with* Hippolito.

Luff. Hippolito.   *Hip.* My Lord :
Has your good Lordfhip ought to command me in?

Luff. I pre-thee leaue vs.

Hip. How's this? come and leaue vs?   *Luff.* Hippolito.

Hip. Your honor--I ftand ready for any dutious emploiment.

Luff Heart, what makft thou here?

Hip. A pritty Lordly humor :   (honor?
He bids me to bee prefent, to depart ; fome-thing has ftung his

Luff. Bee neerer, draw neerer :
Ye'are not fo good me thinkes, Ime angry with you.

Hip. With me my Lord? Ime angry with my felfe fort.

Luff. You did preferre a goodly fellow to me,
Twas wittily elected, twas, I thought
Had beene a villaine, and he prooues a Knaue?
To mee a Knaue.

Hip. I chofe him for the beft my Lord,
Tis much my forrow, if neglect in him, breed difcontent in you.

Luff. Neglect, twas will : Iudge of it,
Firmely to tell of an incredible Act,
Not to be thought, leffe to be fpoken of,
Twixt my Step-mother and the Baftard, oh,
Inceftuous fweetes betweene 'em.

G

Hip. Fye

Hip. Fye my Lord.

Luſ. I in kinde loyaltie to my fathers fore-head,
Made this a deſperare arme, and in that furie,
Committed treaſon on the lawfull bed,
And with my ſword een rac'd my fathers boſome,
For which I was within a ſtroake of death.

Hip. Alack, Ime ſorry; ſfoote iuſt vpon the ſtroake,
Iars in my brother, twill be villanous Muſick.

Vind My honored Lord.　　　　*Enter* Vind.　　　(thee.

Luſ. Away pre-thee forſake vs, heereafter weele not know

Vind. Not know me my Lord, your Lorſhip cannot chooſe.

Luſ Begon I ſay, thou art a falſe knaue.

Vind. Why the eaſier to be knowne, my Lord.

Luſ. Puſh, I ſhall prooue too bitter with a word,
Make thee a perpetuall priſoner,
And laye this yron-age vpon thee,

Vind Mum, for theres a doome would make a woman dum,
Miſſing the baſtard next him the winde's comes about,
Now tis my brothers turne to ſtay, mine to goe out. *Exit* Vin.

Luſ. Has greatly moou'd me.　　*Hip.* Much to blame ifaith.

Luſ. But ile recouer, to his ruine : twas told me lately,
I know not whether falſlie, that you'd a brother,

Hip. Who I, yes my good Lord, I haue a brother

Luſ. How chance the Court neere ſaw him ? of what nature?
How does he apply his houres ?

Hip. Faith to curſe Fates,
Who, as he thinkes, ordaind him to be poore,
Keepes at home full of want and diſcontent.

Luſ There's hope in him, for diſcontent and **want**
Is the beſt clay to mould, a villaine off;
Hippolito, wiſh him repaire to vs
If there be ought in him to pleaſe our bloud,
For thy ſake weele aduance him, and build faire
His meaneſt fortunes : for it is in vs
To reare vp Towers from cottages.

Hip. It is ſo my Lord, he will attend your honour,
But hees a man, in whom much melancholy dwels.

Luſ. Why the better : bring him to Court.

Hip.

Hip. With willingneſſe and ſpeed,
Whom he caſt off een now, muſt now ſucceed,
Brother diſguiſe muſt off,
In thine owne ſhape now, ile prefer thee to him :
How ſtrangely does himſelfe worke to vndo him.   *Exit.*

   Luſſ. This fellow will come fitly, he ſhall kill,
That other ſlaue, that did abuſe my ſpleene,
And made it ſwell to Treaſon, I haue put
Much of my heart into him, hee muſt dye.
He that knowes great mens ſecrets, and proues ſlight,
That man nere liues to ſee his Beard turne white :
I he ſhall ſpeede him : Ile employ thee brother,
Slaues are but Nayles, to driue out one another?
Hee being of black condition, ſutable
To want and ill content, hope of preferment
Will grinde him to an Edge——The Nobles enter.

   1. Good dayes vnto your honour.
   Luſſ. My kinde Lords, I do returne the like.
   2. Sawe you my Lord the Duke ?
   Luſſ. My Lord and Father, is he from Court?
   1. Hees ſure from Court,
But where, which way, his pleaſure tooke we know not,
Nor can wee heare ont.
   Luſſ. Here come thoſe ſhould tell,
Sawe you my Lord and Father?
   3. Not ſince two houres before noone my Lord,
And then he priuately ridde forth.
   Luſ. Oh hees rod forth.
   1. Twas wondrous priuately,
   2. Theres none ith Court had any knowledge ont.
   Luſ. His Grace is old, and ſudden, tis no treaſon
To ſay, the Duke my Father has a humor,
Or ſuch a Toye about him ; what in vs
Would appeare light, in him ſeemes vertuous.
   3. Tis Oracle my Lord.   *Exeunt.*
   Enter Vindice *and* Hippolito, Vind. *out of his diſguiſe.*
   Hip. So, ſo, all's as it ſhould be, y'are your ſelfe.
   Vind. How that great-villaine puts me to my ſhifts.

     Hip.

Hip. Hee that did lately in difguize reiect thee ;
Shall now thou art thy felfe, as much refpect thee.

Vind. Twill be the quainter fallacie ; but brother,
Sfoote what vfe will hee put me to now thinkft thou ?

Hip. Nay you muft pardon me in that, I know not :
H'as fome employment for you : but what tis
Hee and his Secretary the Diuell knowes beft.

Vind, Well I muft fuite my toung to his defires,
What colour fo ere they be ; hoping at laft
To pile vp all my wifhes on his breft,

Hip. Faith Brother he himfelfe fhowes the way.

Vind. Now the Duke is dead, the realme is clad in claye :
His death being not yet knowne, vnder his name
The people ftill are gouernd; well, thou his fonne
Art not long-liu'd, thou fhalt not ioy his death :
To kill thee then, I fhould moft honour thee ;
For twould ftand firme in euery mans beliefe,
Thou'ft a kinde child, and onely dyedft with griefe.

Hip. You fetch about well, but lets talke in prefent,
How wil you appeare in fafhion different,
As well as in apparrell, to make all things poffible :
If you be but once tript, wee fall for euer.
It is not the leaft pollicie to bee doubtfull,
You muft change tongue:--familiar was your firft.

Vind. Why he beare me in fome ftraine of melancholie,.
And ftring my felfe with heauy--founding Wyre,
Like fuch an Inftrument, that fpeakes merry things fadly.

Hip. Then tis as I meant,
I gaue you out at firft in difcontent.

Vind. Ile turne my feife, and then ——— —

Hip. Stoote here he comes : haft thought vppont.

Vind. Salute him, feare not me.   *Luff.* Hippolito.

Hip. Your Lordfhip.   *Luff.* What's he yonder ?

Hip. Tis *Vindici*, my difcontented Brother,
Whom, cording to your will I'aue brought to Court.

Luff, Is that thy brother? befhrew me, a good prefence,
I wonder h'as beene from the Court fo long ?
Come neerer.

Hip. Brother, Lord *Luſſurioſo* the Duke ſonne.   *Snatches of*
Luſſ. Be more neere to vs, welcome, neerer yet.   *his hat and*
Vind. How don you god you god den.   *makes legs*
Luſſ. We thanke thee?   *to him.*
How ſtrangly ſuch a courſe-homely ſalute,
Showes in the Pallace, where we greete in fire:
Nimble and deſperate tongues, ſhould we name,
God in a ſalutation, twould neere be ſtood on't,—heauen!
Tell me, what has made thee ſo melancholy.

Vind. Why, going to Law.

Luſſ. Why will that make a man mellancholy?

Vind. Yes, to looke long vpon inck and black buckrom—I
went mee to law in *Anno Quadrageſimo ſecundo*, and I waded
out of it, in *Anno ſextageſimo tertio.*

Luſſ. What, three and twenty years in law?

Vind. I haue knowne thoſe that haue beene fiue and fifty, and
all about Pullin and Pigges.

Luſſ. May it bee poſſible ſuch men ſhould breath,
To vex the Tearmes ſo much. *Vin.* Tis foode to ſome my Lord.
There are olde men at the preſent, that are ſo poyſoned
with the affectatió of law-words, (hauing had many ſuites can-
uaſt,) that their common talke is nothing but Barbery lattin:
they cannot ſo much as pray, but in law, that their ſinnes may
be remou'd, with a writ of Error, and their ſoules fetcht vp to
heauen, with a ſaſarara.

Hip. It ſeemes moſt ſtrange to me,
Yet all the world meetes round in the ſame bent:
Where the hearts ſet, there goes the tongues conſent,
How doſt apply thy ſtudies fellow?

Vind. Study why to thinke how a great rich man lies a dying,
and a poore Cobler toales the bell for him? how he cannot de-
part the world, and ſee the great cheſt ſtand before him, when
hee lies ſpeechleſſe, how hee will point you readily to all the
boxes, and when hee is paſt all memory, as the goſſeps geſſe,
then thinkes hee of forffetures and obligations, nay when to all
mens hearings he whurles and rotles in the throate hee's buſ-
ſie threatning his poore Tennants? and this would laſt me now
ſome ſeauen yeares thinking or there abouts? but, I haue a

    conceit

Conceit a comming in picture vpon this, I drawe it my selfe,
which ifaith Ia Ile prefent to your honor, you fhall not chofe
but like it for your Lordfhip fhall giue me nothing for it,

*Luff.*Nay you mifstake me then,
For I am publifht bountifull inough,
Lets taft of your conceit.

Vin In picture my Lord.   *Luff.*I in picture,

Vin. Marry this it is——*A vfuring Father to be boyling in hell,
and his fonne and Heire with a Whore dancing ouer him.*

*Hip.*Has par'd him to the quicke.

*Luf.*The conceit's pritty ifaith,
But tak't vpon my life twill nere be likt.

Vind. No, why Ime fure the whore will be likt well enough.

*Hip.*I if fhe were out ath picture heede like her then himfelfe.

*Vin.*And as for the fonne and heire,he fhall be an eyefore to
no young Reuellers,for hee fhall bee drawne in cloth of **gold**
breeches.

*Luff.*And thou haft put my meaning in the pock,
And canft not draw that out,my thought was this, ets
To fee the picture of a vfuring father
Boyling in hell,our richmen would nere like it,

Vin. O true I cry you heartly mercy I hnow **the reafon,** for
fome of'em had rather be dambd indeed,thē dambd in **colours.**

*Luf.*A parlous melancholy,has wit enough,
To murder any man,and Ile giue him meanes,
I thinke thou art ill monied;

*Vin.*Money,ho,ho,
Tas beene my want fo long,tis now my fcoffe.
Iue ene forgot what colour filuers off,

Luf It hits as I could wifh,   *Vin.*I get good **cloths,**
Of thofe that dread my humour,and for table-roome,
I feed on thofe that cannot be rid of me,

*Luf.*Somewhat to fet thee vp withall,

*Vin.*O mine eyes,   *Luf.*How now man.

*Vin.*Almoft ftrucke blind,
This bright vnufuall fhine,to me feemes proud,
I dare not looke till the funne be in a cloud,

*Luf.*I thinke I fhall afecte his melancholy,

How

How are they now.   *Vin.* The better for you rasking.

Luſ. You ſhall be better yet if you but faſten,
Truly on my intent, now yare both preſent
I will vnbrace ſuch a cloſſe priuate villayne,
Vnto your vengfull ſwords, the like nere heard of,
Who hath diſgrac'd you much and iniur'd vs,

Hip. Diſgraced vs my Lord?

Lnſ.! *Hippolito.*
I kept it here till now that both your angers,
Might meete him at once,

Vin. Im e couetuous,
To know the villayne,

Luſ. You know him that ſlaue Pandar,
Piato whome we threatened laſt
With irons in perpetuall priſonment;

Vin. All this is I.   *Hip.* Iſt he my Lord?

Luſ. Ile tell you, you firſt preferd him to me.

Vin. Did you brother.   *Hip.* I did indeed?

Luſ. And the ingreatfull villayne,
To quit that kindnes, ſtrongly wrought with me,
Being as you ſee a likely man for pleaſure,
With iewels to corrupt your virgin ſiſter.

Hip. Oh villaine,   *Vin.* He ſhall ſurely die that did it.

Luſ. I far from thinking any Virgin harme,
Eſpecially knowing her to be as chaſt
As that part which ſcarce ſuffers to be toucht,
Th' eye would not endure him,

Vin. Would you not my Lord,
Twas wondrous honorably donne,

Luſ. But with ſome fiue fro vnes kept him out,

Vin. Out ſlaue.

Luſ. What did me he but in reuenge of that,
Went of his owne free will to make infirme,
Your ſiſters honor, whome I honor with my ſoule,
For chaſt reſpect, and not preuayling there,
(As twas but deſperate folly to attempt it,)
In meere ſpleene, by the way, way laies your mother,
Whoſe honor being a coward as it ſeemes,

                                        Yeelded

Yeelded by little force.   *Vind.* Coward indeed.

Luss. He proud of their aduantage, (as he thought)
Brought me these newes for happy , but I , heauen forgiue mee
Vind. What did your honour.   (for't.

Luss. In rage pusht him from mee,
Trampled beneath his throate, spurnd him, and bruizd :
Indeed I was too cruell to say troth.

 Hip. Most Nobly managde.

 Vind. Has not heauen an eare? Is all the lightning wasted?

 Luss. If I now were so impatient in a modest cause,
What should you be?

 Vind. Full mad, he shall not liue
To see the Moone change.

 Luss. He's about the Pallace,
Hippolito intice him this way, that thy brother·
May take full marke of him.

 Hip. Heart?—that shall not neede my Lord,
I can direct him so far.

 Luss Yet for my hates sake,
Go, winde him this way: ile see him bleede my selfe.

 Hip. What now brother?

 Vind. Nay e'en what you will— y'are put to't brother?

 Hip. An impossible taske, Ile sweare,
To bring him hither, thats already here. *Exit* Hippo.

 Luss. Thy name, I haue forgot it? *Vin.* Vindice my Lord.

 Luss. Tis a good name that. *Vind.* I, a Reuenger.

 Luss. It dos betoken courage, thon shouldst be valiant,
And kill thine enemies. *Vind.* Thats my hope my Lord.

 Luss. This slaue is one. *Vind.* Ile doome him.

 Luss. Then ile praise thee?
Do thou obserue me best, and Ile best raise thee. *Enter.* Hip.

 Vind Indeed, I thanke you.

 Luss. Now Hippolito, where's the slaue Pandar?

 Hip. Your good Lordship,
Would haue a loathsome sight of him, much offensiue?
Hee's not in case now to be seene my Lord,
The worst of all the deadly sinnes is in him:
That beggerly damnation, drunkennesse.

            Luss.

Luſſ. Then he's a double-ſlaue.

Vind. Twas well conuaide, vpon a ſuddaine wit.

Luſſ. What, are you both,
Firmely reſolud, ile ſee him dead my ſelfe.

Vind. Or elſe, let not vs liue.

Luſſ. You may direct your brother to take note of him.

Hip. I ſhall.

Luſſ. Riſe but in this, and you ſhall neuer fall.

Vind. Your honour: Vaſſayles.

Luſſ. This was wiſely carried,
Deepe policie in vs, makes fooles of ſuch:
Then muſt a ſlaue die, when he knowes too much.   *Exi.* Luſſ.

Vind. O thou almighty patience, tis my wonder,
That ſuch a fellow, impudent and wicked,
Should not be clouen as he ſtood:
Or with a ſecret winde burſt open!
Is there no thunder left, or iſt kept vp
In ſtock for heauier vengeance, there it goes!

Hip. Brother we looſe our ſelues ?

Vind. But I haue found it,
Twill hold, tis ſure, thankes, thankes to any ſpirit,
That mingled it mongſt my inuentions.

Hip. What iſt?

Vind. Tis found, and good, thou ſhalt pertake it,
I'me hir'd to kill my ſelfe.   *Hip.* True.

Vind. Pree-thee marke it,
And the old Duke being dead, but not conuaide,
For he's already miſt too, and you know:
Murder will peepe out of the cloſeſt huſke.   *Hip.* Moſt true?

Vind. What ſay you then to this deuice,
If we dreſt vp the body of the Duke.

Hip. In that diſguiſe of yours.

Vind. Y'are quick, y'aue reacht it.

Hip. I like it wonderouſly.

Vind. And being in drinck, as you haue publiſht him,
To leane him on his elbowe, as if ſleepe had caught him:
Which claimes moſt intereſt in ſuch ſluggy men.

Hip. Good yet, but here's a doubt,

H   **Me**

Me thought by'th Dukes sonne to kill that pandar,
Shall when he is knowne be thought to kill the Duke.

    Vind. Neither, O thankes, it is substantiall
For that disguize being on him, which I wore,
It wil be thought I, which he calls the Pandar, did kil the Duke,
& fled away in his apparell, leauing him so disguiz'd, to auoide
swift pursuite   *Hip.* Firmer, and firmer.

    Vind. Nay doubt not tis in graine, I warrant it hold collour.

    Hip. Lets about it.

    Vind. But by the way too, now I thinke on'r, brother,
Let's coniure that base diuill out of our Mother.   *Exeunt.*

*Enter the Dutches arme in arme with the Bastard: he seemeth lasci-
uiously to her, after them, Enter* Superuacuo, *running with a ra-
pier, his Brother stops him.*

    Spuri. Madam, vnlock your selfe, snould it be seene,
Your arme would be suspected.

    Duch. Who ist that dares suspect, or this, or these?
May not we deale our fauours where we please?

    Spu. I'me, confident, you may.   *Exeunt.*

    Amb. Sfoot brother hold.

    Sup. Woult let the Bastard shame vs?

    Amb. Hold, hold, brother? there's fitter time then now.

    Sup. Now when I see it.   *Amb.* Tis too much seene already.

    Sup. Seene and knowne,
The Nobler she's, the baser is shee growne.

    Amb. If she were bent lasciuiously, the fault
Of mighty women, that sleepe soft, -- O death,
Must she needes chuse such an vnequall sinner:
To make all worse.

    Sup. A Bastard, the Dukes Bastard, Shame heapt on shame.

    Amb. O our disgrace.
Most women haue small waste the world through-out,
But there desires are thousand miles about.   *Exeunt.*

    Sup. Come stay not here, lets after, and preuent,
Or els theile sinne faster then weele repent.

Enter Vindice *and* Hippolito, *bringing out there Mother
one by one shoulder, and the other by the other, with
daggers in their hands.*

                       Vind.

Vind. O thou? for whom no name is bad ynough.

Moth. What meanes my sonnes what will you murder me?

Vind. Wicked vnnaturall Parents.

Hip. Feend of women.

Moth. Oh! are sonnes turnd monsters? helpe.

Vind. In vaine.

Moth. Are you so barbarous to set Iron nipples
Vpon the brest that gaue you suck.

Vind. That brest,
Is turnd to Quaried poyson.

Moth. Cut not your daies for't. am not I your mother?

Vind. Thou dost vsurpe that title now by fraud
For in that shell of mother breeds a bawde.

Moth. A bawde? O name far loathsomer then hell.

Hip. It should be so knewst thou thy Office well.

Moth. I hate it.

Vind. Ah ist possible, *Thou onely,* you powers on hie,
That women should dissemble when they die.

Mot. Dissemble.

Vind. Did not the Dukes sonne direct
A fellow, of the worlds condition, hither,
That did corrupt all that was good in thee:
Made thee vnciuilly forget thy selfe,
Aud worke our sister to his lust.

Moth. Who I,
That had beene monstrous? I defie that man:
For any such intent, none liues so pure,
But shall be soild with slander, —good sonne beleiue it not,

Vind. Oh I'me in doubt,
Whether I'me my selfe, or no,
Stay, let me looke agen vpon this face.
Who shall be sau'd when mothers haue no grace.

Hip. Twould make one halfe dispaire.

Vind. I was the man,
Defie me, now? lets see, do't modestly.

Moth. O hell vnto my soule.

Vind. In that disguize, I sent from the Dukes sonne,
Tryed you, and found you base mettell,

As

As any villaine might haue donne.

Mo. O no,no tongue but yours could haue bewitcht me so.

Vind. O nimble in damnation, quick in tune,
There is no diuill could ftrike fire fo foone:
I am confuted in a word.

Mot. Oh fonnes , forgiue me,to my felfe ile proue more true,
You that fhould honor me,I kneele to you.

Vind. A mother to giue ayme to her owne daughter.

Hip. True brother,how far be yond nature 'tis,
Tho many Mothers do't.

Vind. Nay and you draw teares once,go you to bed,
Wet will make yron blufh and change to red:
Brother it raines,twill fpoile your dagger,houfe it.

Hip Tis done.

Vin. Yfaith tis a fweete fhower, it dos much good,
The fruitfull grounds,and meadowes of her foule,
Has beene long dry:powre downe thou bleffed dew,
Rife Mother , troth this fhower has made you higher.

Mot. O you heauens?take this infectious fpot out of my foule,
Ile rence it in feauen waters of mine eyes?
Make my teares falt ynough to taft of grace,
To weepe,is to our fexe:naturally giuen:
But to weepe truely thats a gift from heauen?

Vind. Nay ile kiffe you now:kiffe her brother?
Lets marry her to our foules,wherein's no luft,
And honorably loue her.   *Hip.* Let it be.

Vind. For honeft women are fo fild and rare,
Tis good to cherifh thofe poore few that are.
Oh you of eafie waxe,do but imagine
Now the difeafe has left you,how leproufly
That Office would haue cling'd vnto your forehead,
All mothers that had any gracefull hue,
Would haue worne mafkes to hide their face at you:
It would haue growne to this , at your foule name;
Greene-collour'd maides would haue turnd red with fhame?

Hip. And then our fifter full of hire,and baffeneffe.

Vind. There had beene boyling lead agen,
The dukes fonnes great Concubine:
A drab of State,a cloath a filuer flut,

To

To haue her traine borne vp,and her soule traile i'th durt ; great.

Hip. To be miserably great,rich to be eternally wretched.

Vind. O common madnesse :
Aske but the thriuingst harlot in cold bloud,
Sheed giue the world to make her honour good,
Perhaps youle say but onely to'th Dukes sonne,
In priuate ; why,shee first begins with one,
Who afterward to thousand prooues a whore :
,,Breake Ice in one place,it will crack in more.

Mother. Most certainly applyed ?

Hip. Oh Brother,you forget our businesse.

Vind. And well remembred,ioye's a subtill elfe,
I thinke man's happiest,when he forgets himselfe :
Farewell once dryed,now holy-watred Meade,
Our hearts weare Feathers,that before wore Lead.

Mother. Ile giue you this,that one I neuer knew
Plead better,for,and gainst the Diuill,then you.

Vind. You make me proud ont.

Hip. Commend vs in all vertue to our Sister.

Vind. I for the loue of heauen,to that true maide.

Mother. With my best words.

Vind. Why that was motherly sayd.   *Exeunt.*

Mother. I wonder now what fury did transport me?
I feele good thoughts begin to settle in me,
Oh with what fore-head can I looke on her ?
Whose honor I'ue so impiouslie beset,
And here shee comes,

Cast. Now mother,you haue wrought with me so strongly,
That what for my aduancement,as to calme
The trouble of your tongue : I am content.

Mother. Content,to what ?

Cast. To do as you haue wisht me,
To prostitute my brest to the Dukes sonne : :
And put my selfe to common Vsury.

Mother. I hope you will not so.

Cast. Hope you I will not ?
That's not the hope you looke to be saued in.

Mother. Truth but it is.

Cast. Do not deceiue your selfe,
I am, as you een out of Marble wrought,
What would you now, are yee not pleasde yet with me,
You shall not wish me to be more lasciuious
Then I intend to be.   *Mother.* Strike not me cold,

Cast. How often haue you chargd me on your blessing
To be a cursed woman---when you knew,
Your blessing had no force to make me lewd,
You laide your cursse vpon me, that did more,
The mothers curse is heauy, where that fights,
Sonnes set in storme, and daughters loose their lights?

Moth. Good childe, deare maide, if there be any sparke
Of heauenly intellectuall fire within thee, oh let my breath,
Reuiue it to a flame :
Put not all out, with womans wilfull follyes,
I am recouerd of that foule disease
That haunts too many mothers, kinde forgiue me,
Make me not sick in health? ---if then
My words preuailde when they were wickednesse,
How much more now when they are iust and good?

Cast. I wonder what you meane, are not you she
For whose infect perswasions I could scarce
Kneele out my prayers, and had much adoo
In three houres reading, to vntwist so much
Of the black serpent, as you wound about me.

Moth. Tis vnfruitfull, held tedious to repeate whats past,
Ime now your present Mother.   *Cast.* Push, now 'tis too late,

Moth. Bethinke agen, thou knowst not what thou sayst.

Cast. No, deny aduancement, treasure, the Dukes sonne.

Moth. O see, I spoke those words, and now they poyson me:
What will the deed do then?
Aduancement, true : as high as shame can pitch,
For Treasure ; who ere knew a harlot rich?
Or cou'd build by the purchase of her sinne,
An hospitall to keepe their bastards in :   The Dukes sonne,
Oh when woemen are yong Courtiers, they are sure to be old
To know the miseries most harlots taste,   (beggars,
Thoudst wish thy selfe vnborne, when thou art vnchast.

Cast. O mother let me twine about your necke,

And

And kiſſe you till my ſoule melt on your lips,
I did but this to trie you.   *Mot.*O ſpeake truth.

    *Caſt.*Indeed I did not,for no tong has force to alter me from
If maydens would,mens words could haue no power,   (honeſt
A vergin honor is a chriſtall Tower.
Which being weake is guarded with good ſpirits,
Vntill ſhe baſely yeelds no ill inherits.

    *Mot.*O happy child!faith and thy birth hath ſaued me,
Mongſt thouſand daughters happieſt of all others,
Buy thou a glaſſe for maides,and I for mothers.   *Exeunt.*

                Enter Vindice *and* Hippolito.

    *Vin.*So,ſo,he leanes well,take heede you wake him not bro-
*Hip.*I warant you my life for yours.   (ther
    *Vin.*Thats a good lay,for I muſt kill my ſelfe?
Brother thats I:that ſits for me:do you marke it,
And I muſt ſtand ready here to make away my ſelfe yonder---I
muſt ſit to bee kild , and ſtand to kill my ſelfe , I could varry it
not ſo little as thrice ouer agen , tas ſome eight returnes like
Michelmas Tearme.   *Hip.* Thats enow a conſcience.

    Vind. But ſirrah dos the Dukes ſonne come ſingle?
Hip. No,there's the hell on't,his faith's too feeble to go alone?
hee brings fleſh-flies after him , that will buzze againſt ſupper
time,and hum for his comming out.

    Vind. Ah the fly-flop of vengeance beate 'em to peeces? here
was the ſweeteſt occaſion , the fitteſt houre , to haue made my
reueng familiar with him , ſhow him the body of the Duke his
father , and how quaintly he died like a Politician in hugger-
mugger,made no man acquainted with it , and in Cataſtrophe
ſlaine him ouer his fathers breſt,and oh I'me mad to looſe ſuch a
ſweete opportunity.

    Hip. Nay puſh , pree-thee be content ! there's no remedy pre-
ſent,may not hereafter times open in as faire faces as this.

    Vind. They may if they can paint ſo well?
Hip. Come,now to auoide al ſuſpition,lets forſake this roome,
and be going to meete the Dukes ſonne.   (comes? *Ent.*Luſſ.
    *Vind.*Content,I'me for any wether ? heart ſtep cloſſe,here hee
Hip. My honord Lord?   *Luſ.*Oh me;you both preſent.
    Vin. E'en newly my Lord,iuſt as your Lordſhip enterd now?a-
bout this place we had notice giuen hee ſhould bee,but in ſome
loathſome plight or other.   *Hip.*

Hip. Can e your honour priuate?

Luss. Priuate inough for this : onely a few
Attend my comming out.   *Hip.* Death rotte those few.

Luss. Stay yonder's the slaue.

Vind. Masse there's the slaue indeed my Lord ;
Tis a good child,he calls his Father slaue.

.Luss. I, thats the villaine,the dambd villaine : softly,
Tread easie.

Vin. Puh,I warrant you my Lord,weele stifsle in our breaths.

Luss. That will do well :
Base roague,thou sleepest thy last,tis policie,
To haue him killd in's sleepe,for if he wakt
Hee would betray all to them.

Vind. But my Lord.   *Luss.* Ha,what sayst?

Vind. Shall we kill him now hees drunke? *Lus.* I best of all.

Vind. Why then hee will nere liue to be sober ?

Lus. No matter,let him reele to hell.

Vind. But being so full of liquor, I feare hee will put out all

Lus. Thou art a mad brest.   (the fire,

Vin. And leaue none to warme your Lordships Gols withall;
For he that dyes drunke,falls into hell fire like a Bucket a water,
qush,qush.

Lus. Come be ready, nake your swords,thinke of your wrongs
This slaue has iniur'd you.

Vind. Troth so he has,and he has paide well fort.

Lus. Meete with him now.

Vin. Youle beare vs out my Lord ?

Lus. Puh,am I a Lord for nothing thinke you,quickly,now.

Vind. Sa,sa,sa : thumpe,there he lyes.

Lus. Nimbly done,ha ? oh,villaines,murderers,
Tis the old Duke my father.   *Vind.* That's a iest.

Lus. What stiffe and colde already ?
O pardon me to call you from your names :
Tis none of your deed, --that villaine *Piato*
Whom you thought now to kill,has murderd him,
And left him thus disguizd.   *Hip.* And not vnlikely.

Vind. O rascall was he not ashamde,
To put the Duke into a greasie doublet.

                                                        Luss.

Luſſ. He has beene cold and ſtiff who knowes, how long?

Vind. Marry that do I.

Luſſ. No words I pray, off any thing entended:

Vind. Oh my Lord.

Hip. I would faine haue your Lordſhip thinke that we haue ſmall reaſon to prate.

Luſ Faith thou ſayſt true? ile forth-with ſend to Court,
For all the Nobles, Baſtard, Ducheſſe, all?
How here by miracle wee found him dead,
And in his rayment that foule villaine fled.

Vind. That will be the beſt way my Lord, to cleere vs all: lets caſt about to be cleere.

Luſſ. Ho, Nencio, Sordido, and the reſt.   *Enter all.*

1. My Lord.   2. My Lord.

Luſ. Be wittneſſes of a ſtrange ſpectacle:
Chooſing for priuate confeſ.ence that ſad roome
We found the Duke my father gealde in b!oud.

1. My Lord the Duke---run hiethee Nencio,
Startle the Court by ſignifying ſo much.

Vind. Thus much by wit a deepe Reuenger can:
When murders knowne, to be the cleereſt man
We're ſordeſt off, and with as bould an eye,
Su. uay his body as the ſlanders by.

Luſſ. My royall father, too baſely let bloud,
By a maleuolent ſlaue.

Hip. Harke? he calls thee ſlaue agen.   *Vin.* Ha's loſt, he may.

Luſ. Oh ſight, looke hether, ſee, his lips are gnawn with poyſó.

Vin. How--his lips by'th maſſe they bee.

Luſ. O villaine -O roague--O ſlaue--O raſcall:

Hip. O good deceite, he quits him with like tearmes.

1. Where.   2. Which way.

Amb. Ouer what roofe hangs this prodigious Comet,
In deadly fire.

Luſ. Behold, behold my Lords the Duke my fathers murderd
by a vaſſaile, that owes this habit, and here left diſguiſde.

Duch. My Lord and huſband.   2. Reuerend Maieſty.

1. I haue ſeene theſe cloths, often attending on him.

Vin. That Nobleman, has bin ith Country, for he dos not lie?

I   *Sup*

Sup. Learne of our mother lets diffemble to,
I am glad hee's vanifht; fo I hope are you?

Amb. I you may take my word fort.

Spur. Old Dad, dead?
I, one of his caft finnes will fend the Fates
Moft hearty commendations by his owne fonne,
Ile tug in the new ftreame, till ftrength be done.

Luf. Where be thofe two, that did affirme to vs?
My Lord the Duke was priuately rid forth?

1. O pardon vs my Lords, hee gaue that charge
Vpon our liues if he were mift at Court,
To anfwer fo; hee rode not any where,
We left him priuate with that fellow here?   *Vind.* Confirmde.

Luf. O heauens, that falfe charge was his death,
Impudent Beggars, durft you to our face,
Maintaine fuch a falfe anfwer? beare him ftraight to execution.

1. My Lord?   *Luff.* Vrge me no more.
In this the excufe, may be cal'd halfe the murther?

Vind. You'ue fentencde well.

Luff. Away fee it be done.

Vind. Could you not ftick: fee what confeffion doth?
Who would not lie when men are hangd for truth?

Hip. Brother how happy is our vengeance.

Vin. Why it hits, paft the apprehenfion of indifferent wits.

Luff. My Lord let poft horfe be fent,
Into all places to intrap the villaine,

Vin. Poft-horfe ha ha.

Neb. My Lord, we're fom-thing bould to know our duety?
Your fathers accidentally departed,
The titles that were due to him, meete you.

Luf. Meete me? I'me not at leifure my good Lord,
I'ue many greefes to difpatch out ath way:
Welcome fweete titles, —talke to me my Lords,
Of fepulchers, and mighty Emperors bones,
Thats thought for me.

Vind. So, one may fee by this,
How forraine markets goe:
Courtiers haue feete ath nines, and tongues ath twellues,

They

They flatter Dukes and Dukes flatter them-selues.

Nob. My Lord it is your shine must comfort vs.

Luss. Alas I shine in teares like the Sunne in Aprill.

Nobl. Your now my Lords grace?

Luss. My Lords grace? I perceiue youle haue it so.

Nobl. 'I is but your owne.

Luss. Then heauens giue me grace to be so?

Vind. He praies wel for him-selfe.

Nobl. Madame all sorrowes,

Must runne their circles into ioyes, no doubt but time,

Wil make the murderer bring forth him-selfe.

Vind. He were an Asse then yfaith?

Nob. In the meane season,

Let vs bethinke the latest-funerall honors:

Due to the Dukes cold bodie,--and withall,

Calling to memory our new happinesse,

Spreade in his royall sonne. ---Lords Gentlemen,

Prepare for Reuells.　　*Vind.* Reuells.

Nobl. Time hath seuerall fals,

Greefes lift vp ioyes, feastes put downe funeralls.

Lus. Come then my Lords, my fauours to you all,

The Duchesse is suspected, fowly bent,

Ile beginne Dukedome with her banishment?　*Exeunt Duke*

Hip. Reuells.　　　　　　　*Nobles and Duckesse.*

Vind. I, that's the word, we are firme yet,

Strike one straine more, and then we crowne our wit. *Exeu.Bro.*

Spu. Well, haue the fayrest marke, --- (so sayd the Duke when

he begot me,)

And if I misse his heart or neere about,

Then haue at any, a Bastard scornes to be out.

Sup. Not'st thou that *Spurio* brother.

And. Yes I note him to our shame.

Super. He shall not liue, his haire shall not grow much longer?

in this time of Reuells tricks may be set a foote, seest thou yon

new Moone, it shall out-liue the new Duke by much, this hand

shall dispossesse him, then we're mighty.

A maske is treasons licence, that build vpon?

Tis murders best face when a vizard's on.　　*Exit Super.*

Amb.

Amb. Ist so, 'ts very good,
And do you thinke to be Duke then, kinde brother:
Ile see faire play, drop one, and there lies tother.   *Exit* Ambi.
          Enter Vindice *&* Hippolito, *with* Piero *and other Lords.*
  Vind. My Lords; be all of Musick, strike old griefes into other
That flow in too much milke, and haue faint liuers, (countries
Not daring to stab home their discontents:
Let our hid flames breake out, as fire, as lightning,
To blast this villanous Dukedome: vext with sinne;
Winde vp your soules to their full height agen.
          Piero. How?   1. Which way?
          3. Any way: our wrongs are such,
We cannot iustly be reuengde too much.
          Vind. You shail haue all enough: ----Reuels are toward,
And those few Nobles that haue long suppressd you,
Are busied to the furnishing of a Maske:
And do affect to make a pleasant taile ont,
The Masking suites are fashioning, now comes in
That which must glad vs all---wee to take patterne
Of all those suites, the colour, trimming, fashion,
E'en to an vndistinguisht hayre almost:
Then entring first, obseruing the true forme,
Within a straine or two we shall finde leasure,
To steale our swords out handsomly,
And when they thinke their pleasure sweete and good,
In midst of all their ioyes, they shall sigh bloud.
          Pie. Weightily, effectually, 3. before the tother Maskers come.
          Vind. We're gone, all done and past.
          Pie. But how for the Dukes guard?   *Vind.* Let that alone,
By one and one their strengths shall be drunke downe,
          Hip. There are fiue hundred Gentlemen in the action,
That will apply them-selues, and not stand idle.
          Pier. Oh let vs hug your bosomes.   *Vin.* Come my Lords,
Prepare for deeds, let other times haue words.   *Exeunt.*
          In a dum shew, the possessing of the young Duke,
               with all his Nobles: Then sounding Musick,
          A furnisht Table is brought forth: then enters the Duke
          & his Nobles to the banquet. A blazing-star appeareth.
                                        Noble-

Noble. Many harmonious houres, and choisest pleasures,
Fill vp the royall numbers of your yeares.

Lus. My Lords we're pleas'd to thanke you?—tho we know,
Tis but your ducty now to wish it so.

Nob. That shine makes vs all happy.

3. *Nob.* His Grace frounes?

2.*Nob.* Yet we must say he smiles.   1.*Nob.* I thinke we must.

Lus. That soule-Incontinent Duchesse we haue banisht,
Tne Bastard shall not liue: after these Reuells
Ile begin strange ones;hee and the stepsonnes,
Shall pay their liues for the first subsidies,
We must not frowne so soone,else t'ad beene now?

1.*Nob.* My gratious Lord please you prepare for pleasure,
The maske is not far off.

Lus. We are for pleasure,
Beshrew thee,what art thou? madst me start?
Thou hast committed treason,---A blazing star.

1,*Nob.* A blazing star, O where my Lord.   *Lus.*Spy out.

2. *Nob,* See,see,my Lords,a wondrous-dreadful one.

Lus. I am not pleas'd at that ill-knotted fire,
That bushing-flaring star,--am not I Duke?
It should not quake me now:had it appeard,
Before it,I might then haue iustly feard,
But yet they say,whom art and learning Weds:
When stars were locks,they threaten great-mens heads,
Is it so ? you are read my Lords.

1.*Nob.* May it please your Grace,.
It showes great anger.

Lus. That dos not please our Grace.

2.*Nob.* Yet here's the comfort my Lord,many times.
When it seemes most it threatnes fardest off.

Lus. Faith and I thinke so too.

1.*Nob.* Beside my Lord,
You'r gracefully establisht with the loues.
Of all your subiects:and for naturall death,
I hope it will be threescore years a comming.

Lus. True , no more but threescore years.

1.*Nob.* Fourescore I hope my Lord: 2,*Nob.*And fiuescore,I,

3,*Nob.*But tis my hope my Lord,you shall nere die.

                                              Lus.

Luf. Giue me thy hand, thefe others I rebuke,
He that hopes fo, is fitteft for a Duke:
Thou fhalt fit next me, take your places Lords,
We're ready now for fports, let 'em fet on.
You things we fhall forget you quite anon!

   3. *Nob.* I heare em comming my Lord.   *Enter the Maske of*
Luf. Ah tis well,   *Reuengers the two Brothers, and*
Brothers, and Baftard, you dance next in hell?   *two Lords more.*

           The Reuengers daunce?
At the end, fteale out their fwords, and thefe foure kill the foure at
        the Table, in their Chaires It thunders.

Vind. Marke, Thunder?
Doft know thy kue, thou big-voyc'ft cryer?
Dukes groanes, are thunders watch-words,
  Hip. So my Lords, You haue ynough.
Vind. Come lets away, no lingring.   *Exeunt.*
Hip. Follow, goe?
Vind. No power is angry when the luft-ful die,
When thunder-claps, heauen likes the tragedy.   *Exit* Vin.
Luf. Oh, oh.
Enter the other Maske of entended murderers, Step-fons, Baftard,
and a fourth man, comming in daunting, the Duke recouers a
little in voyce, and groanes, —calls a guard, treafon.
At which they all ftart out of their meafure, and turning towards
the Table, they finde them all to be murdered.
Spur. Whofe groane was that?   *Luf.* Treafon, a guard.
Amb. How now? all murderd!   *Super.* Murderd!
4. And thofe his Nobles?
Amb. Here's a labour fau'd,
I thought to haue fped him, Sbloud how came this.
Spur. Then I proclaime my felfe, now I am Duke.
Amb Thou Duke,! brother thou lieft.
Spu. Slaue fo doft thou?
4. Bafe villayne haft thou flaine my Lord and Maifter.
         Enter the firft men.
Vind. Piftolls, treafon, murder, helpe, guard my Lord the Duke.
Hip. Lay hold vpon this Traytors?   *Luf.* Oh.
Vind. Alaffe, the Duke is murderd.   *Hip.* And the Nobles.
                                Vind.

Vin Surgeons, Surgeons,--heart dos he breath so long.

Ant. A piteous tragœdy, able to wake,

An old-mans eyes bloud-shot; *Luss.* Oh.

    Vin. Looke to my Lord the Duke-a vengeance throttle him,

Confesse thou murdrous and vnhollowed man,

Didst thou kill all these?

    4. None but the Bastard I,

Vin. How came the Duke slaine then;

    4. We found him so,   *Luss.* O villaine,

Vin. Harke.   *Luss.* Those in the maske did murder vs,

Vin. Law you now sir.

O marble impudence! will you confesse now?

    4. Sloud tis all false,

Ant. Away with that foule monster,

Dipt in a Princes bloud.

    4. Heart tis a lye,

Ant. Let him haue bitter execution.

Vin. New marrow no I cannot be exprest,

How faires my Lord the Duke.

Luss. Farewel to al,

He that climes highest has the greatest fall,

My tong is out of office.

    Vin. Ayre Gentlemen, ayre,

Now thoult not prate ont, twas *Vindice* murdred thee,

    Luss. Oh.   *Vin.* Murdred thy Father.

    Luss. Oh.

    Vin. And I am he-tell no-body, so so, the Dukes departed,

    Ant. It was a deadly hand that wounded him,

The rest, ambitious who should rule and sway,

After his death were so made all away,

    Vin. My Lord was vnlikely,   *Hip.* Now the hope,

Of *Italy* lyes in your reuerend yeares?

    Vin. Your hayre, will make the siluer age agen,

When there was fewer but more honest men,

    Anto. The burdens weighty and will presse age downe,

May I so rule that heauen nay keepe the crowne,

    Vin. The rape of your good Lady has beene quited,

With death on death.   *Ant.* Iust is the Lawe aboue

                                  But

But of al things it puts me most to wonder,
How the old Duke came murdred.   *Vin.* Oh, my Lord.
     Ant. It was the strangeliest carried, I not hard of the like,
     Hip. Twas all donne for the best my Lord,   (now,
     Vin. All for your graces good? we may be bould to speake it
Twas some-what witty carried tho we say it.
Twas we two murdred him,   *Ant.* You two?
     Vin. None else ifaith my Lord nay twas well managde,
     Ant. Lay hands vpon those villaines.   *Vin.* How? on vs?
     Ant. Beare 'em two speedy execution,
     Vin. Heart wast not for your good my Lord?
     Ant. My good away with 'em such an ould man as he,
You that would murder him would murder me,
     Vin. Ist come about;   *Hip.* Sfoote brother you begun,
     Vin. May not we set as well as the Dukes sonne,
Thou hast no conscience, are we not reuengde?
Is there one enemy left aliue amongst those?
Tis time to die, when we are our selues our foes.
When murders shut deeds closse, this curse does seale 'em,
If none disclose 'em they them selues reueale 'em!
This murder might haue slept in tonglesse brasse,
But for our selues, and the world dyed an asse;
Now I remember too, here was *Piato.*   (time
B^ought forth a knauish sentance once, no doubt (said he) but
Will make the murderer bring forth himselfe?
Tis well he died, he was a witch,
And now my Lord, since we are in for euer:
This worke was ours which else might haue beene slipt,
And if we list, we could haue Nobles clipt,
And go for lesse then beggers. but we hate
To b^eed so cowardly we haue ynough,
Yfaith, we're well, our Mother turnd, our Sister true,
We die after a nest of Dukes. adue,   *Exeunt.*
     Ant. How subtilly was that murder closde, beare vp,
Those tragick bodies, tis a heauy season:
Pray heauen their bloud may wash away all treason.   *Exit.*

FINIS.

APPENDIX: PRESS VARIANTS

The following press variants have been detected:

		Uncorrected state	*Corrected state*
A1	imprint	1607	1608
A2v	14 down	laughter	laughter,
A2v	18 down	death	deaths
A4v	6 down	woman are	woman; are
A4v	8 up	well.	well
D4	15 up	Snn	Sun
E3v	9 down	poeple	people
F1	12 down	appoynted:	appoynted
F3	10 down	Father,	Father
F3	16 down	nor	not
G3	19 down	To vex . . . much./	To vex . . . much.
		Vin. Tis . . . at the/	*Vin.* Tis . . . Lord./
H1v	2 down	Shalt	Shall
H1v	8 down	graihe	graine
H1v	6 up	about,	about. *Exeunt.*
H1v	5 up	Or . . . repent. *Exeunt.*	*Sup.* Come . . . preuent
		Sup. Come . . . preuent,	Or . . . repent.
H2	15 down	knowst	knewst
H2	16 up	the	thee
H2	2 up	disguize	disguize,
H2v	9 down	beyond . . . to't	be yond . . . 'tis
H2v	12 down	Wee will make you blush	Wet will make you blush
			Wet will make yron blush
H2v	2 up	Dukes	The dukes
H3	2 down	Too	To be
H4	20 up	faith	faith's
H4	14 up	hee did	he died
H4	4 up	me you	me; you
H4	1 up	leathsome	loathsome
H4v	20 up	beast	brest
H4v	16 up	make	nake

113

I gratefully acknowledge the kindness of Professor George R. Price in providing me with the above list. He also notes a few places in which loosening of the type has affected the printing of some copies: "about" on D3, catchword; "Without" on E1v, catchword; "Mock off thy head." on G1, 6 down; and "pockets" on G3v, 18 down.

The Huntington copy that served as basis for this facsimile prints all variant formes in their press-corrected state. Price collated the two Folger copies, the two Huntington copies, the Childs-Yale copy, and copies at the William Andrews Clark, Boston Public, Harvard, and Chapin libraries. He found that: A(o) and F(o) were uncorrected only in the Childs-Yale copy; the single correction in D(i) occurred in Huntington 1608, Folger 1607, and Chapin; only Harvard had the single variant in E(i) in its uncorrected state; G(o) was uncorrected in the Clark, Boston, and Chapin copies; H(i) and H(o), where the variants are of more interest, divided thus:

	Uncorrected state	Corrected state
H(i)	Huntington 1607	Huntington 1608
	Boston	Clark
	Harvard	Yale
	Chapin	Folger 1607
		Folger 1608
H(o)	Huntington 1607	Huntington 1608
	Yale	Clark
	Folger 1608	Folger 1607
	Boston	
	Harvard	
	Chapin	

However, Boston and Chapin have the one variant on H2v, 12 down, in its intermediate state.